Solution Design

to

Win

Simple Method to Design Large Multi-Million Dollar B2B Business & Technology Solutions so You & Your Customer Both Win

Hassan Nasser
Designing Winning Solutions for 10+ years

Praise for the Book

"Written by a practitioner having been deep in the trenches. The solutions offered in this book are not theoretical but rather cut straight to the chase, ultimately saving time and heartache for those looking to be effective in their deals."

- Reid Anderson - Managing Director, Trestle Innovation

"Hassan's unique methodology in Solutions Design is easy to follow and leaves no deal aspect to luck! I highly recommend to read this book and implement the Simple Solution Framework in your organization."

- Sophie Guibaud - Chief Growth Officer, OpenPayd

"This book covers best practices, tools and insights that are easy to adopt which lets you and your team align and focus on your customer and their objectives without losing sight of your deliverables. The Simple Solution Framework lets you easily differentiate yourself from your competitors throughout your pursuit journey by being more agile and collaborative in your engagements."

- Rajaneesh Kurup - Senior Manager - Solution Marketing, Equinix

"When thinking about Solution Design, Solution Architecture and Sale of multi-million dollar Solutions this book is a must read! The Simple Solution Framework described is easy for anyone to follow and work with on a day-to-day basis to ensure your solution stands out."
- Karim Mourabet - Global Services Principal Consultant, Finastra

"One of the most difficult skills for a sales solutions architect is moving from a good conversation to a sale. Hassan has taken his years of success in this regard and developed a well tested guide with practical examples, great advice and keen insights for taking customers on that journey. This isn't a book for those seeking the most elegant solution; this book is for those seeking the winning solution. With barely a mention of technology, Hassan elucidates how to deliver customer success through business technology solutions, and delivers a methodology for consistently building trust with both internal and external stakeholders. His clear, concise "rules of the road" presented with crystal clarity make this book a must for any sales solutions architect's e-book collection."
- Dan Angelucci - Chief Technology Officer, DXC

"Hassan has personally lived and breathed the content while successfully leading multi-million solution deals making this book absolutely real and credible. He brings the relevant factors together into a practical straightforward framework which should be considered by anyone involved in such sales processes and interested in getting more results or getting better at it."
- Michael Schmale - former Chief Delivery Officer, Fidor Solutions

"The Simple Solution Design Framework gives you the platform and tools to build winning solutions time and time again. This process ensures that even with solutions that incorporate tens,or hundreds of stakeholder, the end result is a deal which is a win-win for you and the client."

- Max Johnson - Head of Business Solution Consulting, Fidor Solutions

"This book reflects the complete hybrid between Business & Technical aspects of Solutioning that enables a platform for aspiring and existing sales professionals to zone in on how to develop and improve on their approach to complex sales in the B2B world."

- Matthew Nicholls - Head of Business Development, Fidor Solutions

Notices

Published by Apiot LLC. The author is represented by Apiot LLC. Graphics designed by the author.

Ebook ISBN 978-1-7338632-0-9

Paperback ISBN 978-1-7338632-1-6

Audiobook ISBN 978-1-7338632-2-3

While the author has made every effort to provide accurate Internet addresses at the time of publication, neither the publisher nor the author assumes any responsibility for errors, or for changes that occur after publication. Further, the publisher does not have any control over and does not assume any responsibility for author or third-party websites or their content.

Acknowledgements

This book would not have been possible without the support of many amazing people in my life. First my wife, Nadiia, thank you for being there for me at all times - this book would not exist without you. I want to thank my family - mom, dad, Assil and Firas - for believing in me. Their support throughout the years made this book see the light. To my close friends, I want to thank you for all the encouragement and support you have shown to me throughout this book writing process.

A special shout out to my advisors on this book. These advisors were critical to shaping the book content towards the right audience. I loved the interactions, the feedback and the brutality of the comments from time to time. You can think of the advisors as the mastermind group behind this book. Though I am the author, the advisors played a crucial role in making this book great, relevant, and to the point. Here is a list of the people, titles, and the companies they were working for at the time of writing that book.

- Karim Mourabet - Global Services Principal Consultant, Finastra
- Daniel Angelucci - Chief Technology Officer, DXC
- Raj Kurup - Senior Manager, Equinix
- Wissam Mahfouz - Director Utilities & Infrastructure, Tetra Tech
- Reid Anderson - Managing Director, Trestle DE
- Ed Boyle - CEO, Medici Bank International
- Vineet Chartuverdi - Country Head, Alibaba Cloud
- Matthew Nichols - Head of Business Development, Fidor Solutions
- Yousef-Abdul Qader - Enterprise Accounts, IBM
- Shahrizal Shaharuddin - Senior Consultant & Solutions Leader, DXC
- Dr Greg Kelaart-Courtney - Senior Digital Transformation Executive, Microsoft
- Ziad Kesrouani - Enterprise Account Executive, Dell EMC
- Rudy Kawmi - Sales Manager, Finastra
- Sophie Guibaud - Chief Growth Officer, OpenPayd Vadim Zendejas - Global Cloud Solution Architect Lead, Microsoft
- Michael Schmale - former Chief Delivery Officer, Fidor Solutions
- Frank Brennan - Head of Change & Business Solutions, Bank of Ireland
- Max Johnson - Head of Business Solution Consulting, Fidor Solutions

Finally, to my launch team and self-publishing school community, I say thank you for all your contributions to help me to get to this point. I did not expect it would involve so much work when I decided to write and launch this book. Your presence and continuous support made this endeavor much easier and enjoyable.

Launch Team:

- Cody Smith
- Amin Maalouf
- Ziad Naseriddin
- Germain Bahri
- Benoit Tayyar
- James Brien
- Assyle Nasser
- Joy Roos Sephton
- Elizabeth Means-Binns
- Don Sebastian
- Christina Yin
- Kathy Green Bourque
- Claire Hallinan
- Ron Lang
- Brian Chew
- Monica Rubombora
- Manar A. Lababidi

As for the cover design, I would like to thank Khushnood-ur-Rahman. He works under the ID of 'Klassic Designs' at 99designs.com. Khushnood was extremely accommodating for changes beyond the contest and his response time and quality of work is great. I highly recommend anyone in need of design work to reach out to 'Klassic Designs' at 99designs.com.

I cannot thank everyone enough for believing in me. I had doubts and fears in the face of a new challenge; but I was able to face this project head on and publish this book thanks to the support of my family, my close friends, my advisors, my launch team, my colleagues, and many other communities and groups. This book is by no means a personal effort but rather a team and community effort.

Author's Note

Have you ever thought there could be a different way to make it easier to design solutions to win? To make it a repeatable system to design solutions to win?

For more than a decade, my passion for business and technology pushed me in the search for knowledge. I read an average of more than 20 books a year, 80-90% of which were related to sales, technology, start-ups, B2B (business to business), software development and software technologies.

I was also lucky to work around great people and work with great customers who allowed me to understand better what is needed in the B2B world, especially in the multi-million dollar bids and solutions space.

This book is only possible following many years spent learning, experimenting, and executing the strategies and tactics described herein. Further, it would not have been possible without the mentors, customers, and people I was lucky enough to work with throughout my career.

You will see much inspiration from methods such as Steve Blanks' *Customer Development*, or Eric Ries' *Lean Startup*, Google's *Design Sprints* or other great books, practices, and methodologies. The list is long!

In this book I have organized the available information better, building on the shoulders of giants, in order to serve the purpose of solving for designing large multi-million dollar solutions to win repeatedly.

I hope you enjoy reading this book. If you wish to leave feedback, go to SD2win.com/Feedback. Your unique experiences coming from different backgrounds, geographies, and industries will be very helpful.

Happy reading!

Table of Contents

Section 1: Setting the Scene

1.1 Introduction

Have you ever been on a team that struggled to design a solution? Have you ever developed a solution that failed to get the intended market traction? Have you ever thought there was a different and better way to design solutions to win?

Most solutions proposed to customers often miss the purpose. Many times a proposed solution ends up not meeting the customer's real objectives or does not solve real challenges or deliver Real Business Benefits.

This often results in waste, although we try to convince ourselves otherwise. Trying to re-use some of the work for our next client usually ends up in a vicious viral cycle despite all good intentions.

And I have been there! I spent a lot of time - thousands of hours - and wasted much effort on solving the wrong problems, getting into too many details and losing focus, answering the mail rather than asking the right questions.

But eventually, I noticed a pattern and figured out a system that allowed me to win almost every time I led the creation, architecture, and design of large solutions. I was totally surprised by the power of this system. I taught it to my colleagues and peers that sell large B2B solutions and I almost always received the same feedback - they loved the simplicity and how impactful the system is. So in this book, I want to teach this simple system, that I call the Simple Solution Framework.

In large enterprise B2B deals, winning sales-qualified leads could be anywhere between 20% and 50% depending on industry and company performance based on various research (Check the notes section at the end of this book.) Using the Simple Solution Framework, my winning ratio increased up to 75% at times, and that is huge! That is winning three out of four deals—and if you are in the industry, you know how challenging that is for large multi-million dollar solutions. These increases were all due to identifying a pattern that works consistently and this is the system I share with you here. By the end of this book - when you follow the system - you will be able to design solutions that are positioned to win consistently.

By following this Simple Solution Framework, you will be able to:

- Identify blind spots early
- Focus your effort on high impact activities
- Qualify 10 times better your opportunity
- Play confidently with uncertainty

- Design a solution that is interoperable, deliverable, and adoptable by its users
- Identify and mitigate risks early and often to design solutions that are positioned to win consistently

I am fortunate to have spent my entire career - more than a decade - designing and architecting winning B2B solutions for customers. I failed many times before I figured it out. Now, I am proud to look back and see the solutions I designed are working and delivering Real Business Benefits to customers.

I was also lucky to have worked in companies of different sizes. I designed and delivered solutions varying from slight complexity - hundreds of thousands of dollars of value - to very large and complex - hundreds of millions of dollars. I also have been blessed to be able to learn from my failures and find a pattern that allowed me to win a lot.

A Winning Solution is not only a solution you are able to sell. While a vendor might get away with selling a broken solution, broken solutions don't last because they do not deliver the promised results. This results in the vendor ending up with a problem customer they cannot use as a reference and drains both company's resources. Broken solutions are a race to the bottom. Instead, a Winning Solution is relevant to your customer and delivers results for both your company and your customer, enabling a sustainable future for both firms.

In this system, there are graphs, diagrams, and pictures. While you can learn much simply by reading or listening to the book, it may also be helpful for you to check out the associated material. You can find these graphs, diagrams, and pictures at SD2Win.com/Diagrams.

Is this book for you?

This book is for you if you are participating in sales, design, delivery or operations of large multi-million dollar B2B solutions. Whether you are a stakeholder, a leader, in a supporting role or want to get into a role participating in the design and sale of large multi-million dollar B2B solutions, this book will be insightful, practical and useful for you.

I believe this system could be applied to any industry. It is proven to work for designing Technology, Software, Enterprise Business Applications, and IT Services Solutions in many different industries. If you come from a different background designing different kinds of large multi-million dollar solutions to sell and you find the book useful, I would be happy to hear from you at SD2Win.com/Feedback.

The following topics are also touched upon in this book:

- Storytelling
- Strategic selling
- Tactical selling.

There are lots of books and content available about the above topics. If you are interested in further learning, the following are recommended:

- *The New Strategic Selling* by J. W. Marriott
- *The Challenger Sale Book* by Brent Adamson and Matthew Dixon
- *Selling in a New Market Space Book* by Brian Burns
- *Building a StoryBrand: Clarify Your Message So Customers Will Listen Book* by Donald Miller
- *Made to Stick: Why Some Ideas Survive and Others Die* by Chip Heath

How to get the most out of this book?

To get the most of out of this book I recommend three things:

1. **Learn:** Read the book and understand the framework. Download and review the resources mentioned in the book to understand the framework better. Subscribe to receive the latest articles, artifacts, and resources at SD2Win.com/NewArticles. Some of the articles will provide you with practical elements, examples, sample Solution Artifacts, how to stay organized to win, what tools to use for what, etc. Use them!
2. **Experiment:** Take your solution through the framework as you read this book. Use the resources, the artifacts in the book and the extended links.

3. **Pilot:** Get the Team involved, make The Simple Solution Framework system work for you and your environment!

Now that you know that there is a better way to design solutions, and you know there is a way to win more deals and grow your business, let me walk through why traditional solution design fails. What are the Secret Concepts behind Winning Solutions? And what is this Simple Solution Framework all about?

1.2 Why Most Solutions Fail

What's the difference between a great solution and a Winning Solution? Why is it that a solution you spend a lot of time and effort on does not always win?

In this chapter, we will drill down a bit more on the challenges that we often face with "Great Solutions" that do not win.

The objective of this chapter is not to offer a solution, but to highlight the problem and its impact, and to identify possible root causes. This better understanding of the problem will allow us to better position a solution for the major problems we face.

If you are already aware of the solution design problems and are looking for the answers, you can jump to the following chapters and sections. I do recommend at least skimming through this section to have a better understanding of what the book is "solving for."

Problem 1: Missing the Big Picture

What does "Missing the Big Picture" mean?

Some of the most detrimental problems in solution design are getting into too many details too fast. For example, you start with:

- Trying to solve for every requirement,
- Answering the requirements of compliance matrix spreadsheets,
- Answering what the client has asked for "line by line."

If you did this, you would be starting detailed solution design too early without reflecting on where you are in the sales process, without understanding the overall business context, without understanding the people aspect, without challenging the customer on different aspects and without building credibility. Essentially, you are starting **solution design** without considering the foundation steps which every trained sales or solution professional knows not to do.

Why is "Missing the Big Picture" a problem? What is the impact?

When there is a miss in the understanding of the big picture, often the solution ends up **not** solving for the customer's real business objectives, challenges or aspirations, but rather solving for something else. It may seem like you are solving for actual customer problems, and only when you look back, you find out that you have been "barking up the wrong tree." One of my colleagues used to say "it is like a doctor treating the symptoms instead of the cause of the disease."

In other words, the solution ends up **solving the wrong problem,** and you often lose the deal.

Another result of missing the big picture and getting into too many details is falling into the **product and features mindset.** This mindset is really dangerous and infectious across the team because everyone loves talking about product and features, but that is **not** the big picture. Products and features are at the level of symptoms - not the disease. It is superficial. A significant part of the big picture is your client's business, your client's clients, their challenges, and their aspirations. It is not about products and features nor about technology, no matter what the client directly tells you or writes down in their requirements documents.

With a **product and features mindset**, you will end up being so product and feature focused that you will likely miss the client's real objectives or will not solve real challenges or will not offer Real Business Benefits that the clients are looking for and, as a result, you often lose the deal.

Why does "Missing the Big Picture" happen in the first place?

Unfortunately, missing the big picture is all too common. I have worked with hundreds of experienced professionals, and easily half of those professionals fall into the trap of missing the big picture for all kinds of reasons.

One of those reasons is a misalignment of the different teams involved during the bid cycle. A bid cycle is different to the sales cycle. The bid cycle starts from the time there is an agreement to put a bid forward to the time of actually putting or sending an offer or a proposal with a solution to your client. During the bid cycle, not all team members get to stand in front of the client or have all the important conversations. Bid cycles are typically short in time, which makes it even more difficult to onboard and brief team members about the bid in a quick and effective manner.

What often happens in a bid is that there are a lot of handoffs from one person to the other - For example, from the account manager, to the sales specialist, to the solution architect, to the delivery and operations personnel. Between five to six busy people, with shared resources, you often end up with a "Game of Telephone" problem where not all the team will understand the 'why', not all the team will have the necessary context, and that creates a lot of alignment overheads. You may get a bit of the "blind men describing the elephant."

Another barrier to seeing the big picture is the mindset of "getting stuff done."

So many people have too much on their plate. They are under intense pressure to meet quarterly targets, close a deal, meet other strategic imperatives, pay for their mortgages, and manage other personal demands at home. Sadly, this is when their hard work and good intentions often turn against them. I have seen this happen many times. That is why at every point of time we should ask ourselves if this activity contributes positively to the overall deal. Perhaps what is needed is to take a breather and look at the big picture.

I have been there myself. I took on the challenge to put together a large multi-million dollar solution in a very short timeframe for the scale of the problem at hand - it was only two weeks. The deal was deemed strategic, and the proposal needed to be a binding offer.

We quickly looked at the client business problem at hand, and we focused on what we needed to do to get the deal out of the door internally.

We did many things well. We lined up all internal stakeholders to ensure a smooth workflow through internal processes. We also gathered a very good team with an inspiring "get it done" attitude.

We worked hard to solve the problems we faced, but the solution design team, despite having the best attitude, had skill gaps in understanding the client's business and some of the new technologies required by the client and necessary to the solution. This resulted in technical and pricing challenges.

So what did we do? We pushed through the problem! We pulled 18 to 22-hour workdays, attempting to learn quickly and design a solution under a tight deadline. We were so focused that we were sleeping on the meeting room floor. The 15-minute power naps turned into one to two hours of deep sleep. The team was exhausted and I was exhausted!

And guess what? We, the solution design team, missed the point of the solution! We were lost in the details, working so hard to solve all the problems we were facing that we did not notice we barely skimmed the surface of the initial client problem at hand. We did not spend time interacting with key client stakeholders. We took the client requirements at face value, and we did not develop a deep enough understanding of the current situation and the big picture before going full-steam at designing a great solution.

Here we see that "getting stuff done" effectively can get in the way of designing a solution. It can blind a team or an individual from seeing the big picture.

Bottom Line

These are definitely not the only reasons why people tend to lose sight of the big picture. There are many other reasons not listed here. What is important is that the method I introduce later in the book will help to completely move away from missing the big picture and maximize your chances to win.

Problem 2: Missing the People Aspect of the Solution

What does "Missing the People Aspect of the Solution" mean?

A client in a B2B context is most often a number of people, not one person.

The people who typically impact your sales cycle are people who are hired, fired or measured by the success of your solution. These are individuals who have a lot to gain from your solution's success and a lot on the line from your solution's failure. You can find a list of relevant stakeholders and their role in a buying process at <u>SD2Win.com/TypicalStakeholdersPersonas</u>.

I know this is basic for professional B2B sales or professional technical sales personnel who have been in the business for a while. Nonetheless, I continue to see that the people aspect is not addressed as part of the solution.

Why is "Missing the People Aspect of the Solution" a problem? What is the impact?

Often, the reason why great solutions fail is because the people aspect of the deal is not addressed.

You might say, "hey, this has nothing to do with designing a solution," but it is important to remember that you are dealing with people, human beings, and often multiple stakeholders, which means often different Personal Agendas or Group Agendas will have an impact on your overall solution. If there is alignment on the Group Agenda, i.e. **Organization Agenda** that's great, though in reality it is often not the case and **Personal Agendas** often end up creating unfair biases between one solution and other solutions.

For example, we often face this problem when selling technology-based solutions. Anyone who has been selling large, multi-million technology-based B2B solutions for a while, often encounters one key stakeholder who has a provider or a technology dear to his or her heart; and also has a huge perceived risk associated with changing that provider or technology. Knowing this will create an unfair bias because you can address it in solution design. You can address it by either embedding the vendor as part of your solution or taking extra care to de-risk changing that technology as part of your solution and working hard with that stakeholder to ensure he/she understands it. Not addressing the latter as part of your solution design and interactions would probably guarantee a loss of your solution no matter how many "bells and whistles" your solution has.

Essentially, these individuals could be executive stakeholders who block the progress of the bid, or they could be operational stakeholders who block the delivery of the solutions. Different stakeholders might have opposing **Personal Agendas** despite the shared group objectives, and these political dynamics would not help you or any other vendor succeed easily.

Of course, there are always nuances that you should be aware of, but not addressing a big Personal Agenda for one of the key stakeholders will often mean that you do not have a Winning Solution.

For example, if your solution has a technical component, and you are dealing with a technical buyer, you need to be on the lookout for his or her motivations. Ask yourself the following questions:

- Is he/she interested in learning new technology that can help him/her evolve in the industry? Or satisfy personal curiosity?
- Does he/she like to work with this new technology just for the sake of association with latest technology in the industry?
- Is he/she looking to solve a business problem?
- Is he/she looking to solve a personal problem?
- Is he/she a brand seeker?
- Is this person just learning from you to acquire technical knowledge and has a personal interest to build the solutions themselves?
- Who does he/she report to within the organization? How big is his/her internal influence?
- Does he/she have a technology or provider dear to his or her heart where he/she is personally vested in and

perceives a high risk of change?

I have witnessed many tech stakeholders whose **Personal Agendas** include learning and experimenting with new technology. When you know this Personal Agenda, that will help you design a solution that caters to this. I have seen vendors doing just that, by offering, as part of their solution, access to the latest research or innovations lab, or inviting stakeholders to be part of an innovation club, or by simply offering further training to empower stakeholders to create their experimentation hub. And these vendors won! The key point here is being relevant to what is perceived to be high-value or high-risk by the stakeholder and addressing it as part of your solution.

What is important is **not** to solve for every person but to ensure your solution does not miss critical buyers **real** personal motivations - your solution needs to address and acknowledge the critical buyers' **real** objectives, challenges or aspirations somehow. Sometimes this is expressed as a strong opinion of the vision of the solution by a stakeholder. Addressing the Personal Agenda or that strong opinion of the vision of the solution does not mean giving whatever the client or stakeholder is asking for; but it often means dealing with it, truly listening to the client in order to **understand the situation**, neutralizing it by addressing the intent of the motivation or the strong opinion. It is okay to offer something else as long as it is justified. Not addressing people's **Personal Agendas** or motivators ensures that you do not have a Winning Solution.

Why does "Missing the People Aspect of the Solution" occur in the first place?

The lead person engaging with the customer sometimes focuses a lot on one person at the customer whom he/she is most comfortable talking to, and in doing so loses sight of the rest of the people involved. This is a critical mistake that I see in both beginners and professionals.

The lead person engaging with the client might say it is not feasible to get access to all the key stakeholders, but I believe there is always a way to make this happen. You can follow a stepped approach, where you can ask for access to new people at every stage. One person introduces you to the other within the organization; every conversation is important. If you have a problem getting access to the right people, this is not a book to help with that. You can find a lot of sales books out there that teach you how to get access to the relevant people. A good book on the topic is How to Get a Meeting with Anyone by Stu Hein.

Bottom Line

The problem usually comes when you don't have insights from various people in the organization around **Personal Agendas** and **Organization Agendas.**

So whether you are directly responsible for the relationship with the client or not, you always need to ask about the people involved in the decision or who will be using the solution and all the influencers associated in order to design a solution that fits your prospective Customer's real Objectives. Understanding the buying process and the people aspect of it is KEY for designing a Winning Solution.

Problem 3: Missing Internal Support

What does "Missing Internal Support" mean?

To be clear, in this context **internal support** means internal to the vendor organizations, not the **external** client organization you are selling to.

A lot of internal problems might be the actual reasons why you do not have a Winning Solution, as mainly it is related to selling solutions outside your capability or your partner's spectrum of capability. Internal problems could also include backing from executives without backing from delivery and operations; or a shallow backing from delivery and operations without assessing the delivery or operational impact of the solution.

Another critical internal problem is when the opposite happens, where there is no executive backing to go into that business, but the delivery and operations teams realize they have the capability to sell, deliver, and operate such a solution. It is critical that you manage your stakeholders and get them involved at the right time before you invest too much and get a sudden block from your executives.

Why is "Missing Internal Support" a problem? What is the impact?

If you have executive support without the backing of delivery and operations, you might still get away with selling, but unless delivery and operational capability is uplifted in time for the start of the project or the transition to the operation, then there is a strong likelihood you will end up with a doomed project.

A doomed project is **not** a Winning Solution. Yes, you might have sold, but you no longer have a client, you do not have a reference, and you spent a lot of time and effort on a deal that did not eventually materialize in revenue over the contract duration. That is not winning!

Whatever your primary responsibility might be within your organization, I say everyone's foundation responsibility is to enable or support having the right conversations early, to surface the delivery and operations' challenges and risks early. Of course, you cannot know everything up front, but you can know a lot with a little continuous effort and assessment.

Further, if you have an incentive structure based on revenue, then you will lose your commission or bonus and, along the way, that new house, car, mortgage payment, activity for your kids, or your vacation money. The ripple impact of a doomed project is real on everyone.

In addition, missing executive support will often result in a lot of internal roadblocks along the way and add many hoops to jump through, instead you could spend your time and energy somewhere else. So if you find yourself battling uphill or swimming against the tide, 95% of the time it is a lost battle. The idea is to focus on the customer and what makes an impact on the customer's business. If you are fighting for executive support from your own company, most often there is a bigger internal picture at play, and you do not know the angle. Most often the result of that is not a Winning Solution because it over-stresses the system and shifts the focus to internal executive selling rather than on the customer.

Why does "Missing Internal Support" occur in the first place?

The first problem is when you have executive support without having delivery and operations support. The reasons behind this could be several things:

- You have a gap between the strategic direction of a company, where a company wants to play a role in a certain industry or space and where the company's actual capability is currently in delivery and operations. Maybe everybody shares the ambition and belief but, ultimately, there is no capability or no way to bridge that capability.

- Or, there is just a lack of candor and straight talk within the organization that results in a gap between executive understanding of current capability versus actual capability. While candor and straight talk are one of those things that almost everyone agrees that it is the right thing to do, it is often quite hard to give and receive and only a few engage in this exchange. This problem could be considered a "culture" or a "leadership" challenge.

- Or, organizational problems such as delivery and operations are not represented in the executive community or their respective executives have the wrong incentive structure that drives their behavior in another direction.

These types of problems are easy to solve if everyone - executives, managers, and employees - are moving in the same direction and when everyone's mindset is "how we can" and it is about "Time to Be Ready." Of course, that ties back to leadership and company culture. In reality, often what is required is alignment, a lot of listening and understanding, and then getting everyone moving in the same direction; it is possible, but it is often an uphill battle. Usually, this alignment must start at the top.

On the second problem, missing executive support while having delivery and operations support. This often happens when there is a gap between what executives are thinking and what the team knows. It happens less in more structured organizations and more when there is a looser structure and fewer processes. These problems are solved by connecting the top leadership with the teams executing on the ground, and having the right processes in place.

Bottom Line

The challenge is to surface internal problems. Open conversations, straight talk, and candor, along with a safe, trusting environment, is a great way to surface these problems.

The earlier internal problems surface, the better the conversations your team can have and the better the decisions you can make given the actual situation.

If your solution delivers benefits and it is aligned fully to real customer objectives but does not have internal backing from key stakeholders to support and deliver it successfully, you do **not** have a Winning Solution. Even if you were successful at selling, you would most likely have a doomed project, which in turn does not represent a Winning Solution.

Problem 4: Missing the Client Business Case

What does "Missing the Client Business Case" mean?

Delivering Real Business Benefits should be aligned with what the customers say they want, i.e. customer's requirements, but often it is not. How does this happen?

In practice, what customers really want is:

- Somewhere between the lines of written or stated requirements,
- Usually **not** given to you in writing but somewhere in people's heads when they express their real opinions,
- Existing in some other places, like data or feedback they have collected.

If you simply answer the client's direct and written requirements, it is almost a guaranteed miss of the client business case. The latter might be an overstatement, but in my experience, this is a rule of thumb rather than the exception.

In some cases you can achieve the desired business benefit by solving a different problem altogether from what the clients say they want, or they want to solve. While the objective of this chapter is to detail the problem rather than detail the solution, it is always important to take a step back from the requirements and look at the underlying problem from different angles to achieve the **real** business case.

Another key aspect of the business case is the perceived risks of your solution. Many times the perceived risk is what kills a Winning Solution despite the great reward profile of that solution. The perceived risk of the solution is part of the client business case; you can think of it as a denominator of the result of the business. This is the formula:

Perceived Value = (Business Case Value) / (Perceived Risk)

In this formula:

- The **reward profile** of the solution is expressed as the **Business Case Value**.
- The **Perceived Risk** is a number where the lowest is "1," and because we are talking about perception, it might change from one individual to another or from one small group of people to another. Typically, the higher the risk, the higher the number, and this can be quantified as an actual risk impact or as a score representing the risk impact.
- **Perceived Value** is the ratio between the **Business Case Value** divided by the **Perceived Risk**.

An oversimplified example representing the previous formula is: I want to take orders for critical services online, but I am concerned about its security and online fulfillment. The reward profile as a business case value could be as big as $50 million, but getting hacked or failing to deliver a good experience fulfilling the service may cause me to lose my most valuable customers, and the perceived risk is definitely higher than $100 million.

As you have seen in the prior example, the idea of this formula is simple: the higher the **Perceived Risk**, the lower the **Perceived Value**.

Why is "Missing the Client Business Case" a problem? What is the impact?

There is no solution without risks - the change is too big, the method is too radical, or there is not enough proof of capability, etc. Also, yes, all risks can be mitigated with the right setup, right team, right skills. However, when the fear in the customer's head takes over, the perceived risk will be bigger than the reward, and you may end up with a great solution that is perceived as too **risky** to be a Winning Solution.

When the Perceived Risk is too high, the resulting Perceived Value is near "0," which is why not addressing the Perceived Risk of the solution is equivalent to missing the client's business case altogether.

Another way you can miss the business case is if you end up delivering benefits that are not the right benefits for the customer or do not make an impact on the customer. In both cases, you miss the client business case, and again you end up without a

Winning Solution.

How many times have you built the customer business case as part of your solution and kept track of it? You may have built a value proposition. I have seen many solutions with a lot of value propositions without a true understanding of the customer business case. Often the result of the latter is a lot of value or benefits that look and sound completely logical; but, unfortunately, are not relevant to your client's real needs and not aligned to your client's real and specific business case.

The real business case is often the internal client pitch to their executives on why they should have your solution or any solution. This real business case is what justifies the spend, and the funding from their perspective. Without a business case, you often have no business with this customer.

Why does "Missing the Client Business Case" occur in the first place?

In my experiences, three reasons often come up:

- **First, you put limits on yourself:** The perception that the business case and perceived risk is too hard to build, too time-consuming, or it would be too generic to build the client business case on their behalf. Most of the time it is not hard, it is not generic and yes, you can do it.

- **Second, you have a big skill gap to cover in time:** A possible lack of understanding of the customer industry that makes it even harder to empathize and understand the real drivers behind the client's problems and the actual risks which makes it hard to assess the business case or the perception of the perceived risk

- **Third, you are in love with your own hype:** "Hey, we have a great value proposition." I believe this is an overused cookie-cutter approach that often binds your mindset to an "inside out mode of thinking." This narrows your vision to focus on yourself versus the customer, which means a lack of focus on the client's perceived risks and the impact on the business case. I don't think you should ignore your differentiators that are relevant to the client business case, note them down, draft the business case, and then note their real impact on the business case

Bottom Line

A solution that does not have a relevant rewards profile to the customer is not a Winning Solution.

A solution that does not clearly address risks and balances the Risks and Rewards profile of the solution in view of a client's **real** business case is not a Winning Solution.

Every solution has risks. So going for a lower risk with a lower reward solution is sometimes okay. It is your job to address the risk and to focus on the reward. Otherwise, you may have a great solution, but it will not WIN.

Why Most Solutions Fail - Chapter Summary

The objective of this chapter was not to offer a solution, but to highlight the problem, its impact, and identify possible root causes.

All of the challenges described above could be aligned with one big, yet simple idea; there is no end-to-end thinking around the solution. It starts from the people aspect of the solution in a complex sales process, navigating all the way internally to how this solution will be delivered, operated, and continuously improved over the period of the contract.

The catch is: if you do **not** have a Winning Solution you can say goodbye to your bonus, your commission, your incentive, that extra-curricular activity you wanted to register your kids for, or simply making your ends meet with that extra money.

Now you know in detail the four main problems of solution design:

- First, missing the Big Picture

- Second, missing the people aspect of the solution
- Third, missing Internal Support (Internal to Vendor Organisation)
- And fourth, missing the Client Business (Includes the Perception of the Risk)

These are definitely not all the problems you could fall into. There are many more. In my experience, these are the major problems that often occur and reoccur again and again.

And it is just plain wrong to fall into these problems, to waste so much time and effort while there is a better way to get to a Winning Solution continuously and consistently.

What is the answer to these problems? Is there a magic bullet? Is there a simple system to avoid these pitfalls?

Section 2: The Secret Concepts That Maximize Your Chances to Win!

The following "Secret Concepts" are relevant every time you are pursuing Solution Design to Win. They are simple ideas that are very powerful when applied in the right situation.

So, before using any "Secret Concept" reflect whether this concept applies to your situation or not. I did describe when and how to apply each concept to make it more practical.

We will refer back to these concepts later in this book when we describe The Simple Solution Framework in more detail.

2.1 Secret Concept 1: Steer Away from Talking about the Solution

In this chapter, we will discuss the why, the when, and the how of this concept in the context of solution design.

As a human being, if someone presents us with a problem or challenge, our brains work in a way that tries to link the problem to something we have experienced before and try to come to a solution. This is often our first instinct. It is really easy to follow that instinct and start discussing the solution to the problem, and it is hard to stop this instinct, pause, and listen to better understand the problem at hand.

So why do you want to move the discussion away from the solution?

Although the problem and the solution seem to be super clear in your head, many times this is not the situation with the customer. Many times, you need to walk through with the customer and build credibility by proving that you know their business. I assume you are selling multi-million-dollar solutions, which means if the customer does not trust you, they will **not** spend millions of dollars with you. So, spend some time building credibility and trust by talking about their business a lot and your business a bit.

If you jump to the answer early on and too fast or attempt to teach the customer about their own business, instead of being perceived as a super smart person who knows their business well, you may be perceived as an arrogant person who is teaching the customer how to do their business. Once you have enough credibility with the person, later in the process, you can do this.

Before discussing a solution, you want to understand the surrounding or underlying business concepts and business challenges, business aspirations, business drivers and business impacts.

The latter is far more important than discussing the solution at an Early Stage. If you design a solution without catering for the real business challenges, business aspirations, business objectives then you might end up "Barking up the wrong tree" a.k.a solving the wrong problem for your client.

Here's a simplified example I borrowed from a good friend of mine that illustrates this point:
My friend had a light bulb at his house that wouldn't turn on. It was a spotlight which is difficult to change and was located high up in the ceiling. He called the community electrician to come to fix it.

As soon as the electrician arrived at his house, the electrician said, "Ah, let me change it for you." There was no conversation about the specifics of the problem. The electrician changed it in five minutes and left. "Great," he thought. "This guy is super."

A few days later, the same light bulb stopped working again. My friend called up the same electrician. He came over and said it must have been a faulty light bulb, changed it in five minutes, and left.

Just two days later, the same thing happened again. This time, my friend called a different electrician, one that had been recommended to him.

The new electrician came, had a conversation with my friend, asked him the right questions, did his assessment in the context of the questions he asked, and discovered that the electrical line to the light was faulty due to humidity. In about 45 minutes, he changed the wires and then changed the light bulb. Three years on and my friend still uses and trusts this electrician.

Often people are so much in the details of the solution that they overlook the big picture. You need to be the person who brings that big picture to your client! You have credibility providing solutions to other similar clients, and you can bring benefits from a multi-client experience, which means the solution he/she is thinking about might not be the optimal solution to the situation.

When you drill into the details of the solution at the beginning, you start restricting the actual solution by the boundaries you draw early on. The more you uncover at an Early Stage, the better. And when you talk about the business side, you start picking up on the people involved in the business. If you start uncovering Blind Spots early that will save you a ton of re-work at a later stage. We will talk about Blind Spots a bit later.

Sometimes customers ask questions directly about the solution or have already thought through the problem or aspiration, and the solution is all that he/she wants to talk about. In this situation, listen to understand, but again you need to steer him/her away from talking about the Solution and focus on the Business.

A colleague of mine has a really cool mental model when it comes to steering away from the solution - he suggests you consider yourself a solution therapist. Sit your customer down, and let them talk freely about their challenges and problems. They might ask you about the medication (solution) constantly, or they keep on describing and discussing the medication and the treatment (solution), but you keep telling them that you can only prescribe the medication when you fully understand and assess the situation." Use this mental model or any other mental model that works for you.

Sometimes customers don't want to talk about their problems.

In that case, it is up to you to ask questions to uncover their problems. Of course, you can only do this after you have built some sort of credibility. We will talk about building credibility a bit later in the book.

When is it critical to Steer Away from Talking about the Solution?

At Early Stages during the client discussions, you want to steer the client away from talking about the solution as much as possible.

When I say Early Stages, I mean the first one to five calls and/ or meetings with your contact at a customer, and every time you meet a new person that works for the same customer, you want to focus on the business context discussion before drilling down into the solution.

You may think that not talking about the solution is crazy. It certainly feels counter-intuitive, especially if you really think you know the problem, you see it clearly, you really understand what needs to be done, and you have done it hundreds of times before. It is super clear for you.

But even then, steer away from talking about the solution at an **Early Stage**. Beyond Early Stage, of course, you need to talk about the solution, but that comes later - always reflect on where you are during the sales process or where you are with your audience and act accordingly.

A great video that reflects this concept can be found at SD2Win.com/ItsNotAboutTheNail.

How to practically Steer Away from Talking about the Solution?

How then do you talk about the business? How do you steer the customer away from a solution discussion at an Early Stage? And what do you talk about?

You talk about a trend in his/her industry - enough to create intrigue to buy into your knowledge.

You talk about his/her competitors and their recent projects.

After each statement, you end up with an open-ended question so that your client can talk, and you can listen, take notes and ask another open-ended question.

When the customer asks you directly about the solution, the way to steer him or her away is to talk about the Real Business Challenges, Objectives or Aspirations.

For example:
- A client might say:
  - "We need to make better-informed decisions.

Tell me about your analytics solution."
- You can reply with:
  - "We have a ton of information about analytics and decision-making but to address your question more specifically, you mentioned better-informed decisions - would you define that in more detail? What kind of decisions are we talking about?"

Let us dig into a bit more detail in the anatomy of the response.

1. You acknowledge his/her question
2. You use his/her keywords in your response to augment rapport and show you are listening
3. You ask an open-ended question about the business.

Then you steer away from discussing the solution by asking different types of questions about the business. For example:

"What kind of problems have previously arisen as a result of these kinds of decisions?"

Or

"I believe there would be some business benefits or results out of improving decision-making - what would these be?"
Now you know when to steer away from the solution discussion, you know why it is really important to steer away from the solution discussion early, and you know how to do it.

Don't worry if you do not get it right the first time - it takes some time to master it, and sometimes it is easier to talk about the solution; remember to be self-aware, restrain yourself, focus on listening and understanding. Finally Practice, Practice, Practice! Practice everywhere, anywhere, in your daily conversation with your colleagues, peers, and even in your personal life - try it out.

As a bonus to the book, I have collated a list of statements and questions I usually use to help steer away from a solution discussion too early - just visit SD2Win.com/ToolsToSteerAway-FromTalkingSolution and feel free to use the questions. Don't be limited to the questions on the list, please make them your own, add or remove questions as you see fit.

Bottom Line

Now you know what I mean when I say Steer Away From Talking About the Solution, why it is really important to do that, when to apply it and how to apply it.

2.2 Secret Concept 2: Reflect on Where You Are in the Client Buying Process

In this chapter we will again discuss the why, the how, and the when of this concept in the context of solution design.

Why is it critical to Reflect on where you are in the Client Buying Process?

The act of solving, designing and creating a solution is often motivating and fun. You feel you are doing something good!

At the same time solving for the sake of solving could be a waste of time. Yes, you might tell me it could help sharpen the axes, or it could help train. If that is the objective of why you are pursuing a certain bid, by all means, go ahead and jump into the solution and solve all kinds of problems.

If your objective is to win a bid, then you need to reflect and focus your efforts on what can help you at which stage of the process. Not knowing the buying process and not knowing where you are in it can be disastrous.

A lack of awareness of where the client is in the buying process is like when you want to go from your current Location A to Location B, except you have no idea where your current Location A is, and you keep driving around wasting fuel and hoping to see a sign that says Location B so that you can stop. It is just crazy to do that. You would usually ask people on the road for directions or have a map, Google maps or a GPS at hand.

A lack of awareness of where you are within the client buying process could easily cost you the deal because you wouldn't know that the client is in final negotiations, while you are still beating around the bush.

At best, a lack of awareness of where you are in the client buying process would cost you a lot of resources, investments in time and effort without progressing the deal forward. Back to our analogy, you keep on driving the car around, burning fuel and hoping to see that sign for Location B.

Your actions need to be situational according to where your client is in their buying process to save both your time and the client's time and decide on your best next action 10 times better.

What are the different stages of a Client Buying Process?

Although you can engage with a client at any point in time during the buying process, there is definitely a process that the buyer needs to go through, usually in this order:

1. Pre-Awareness initiation Phase
   a. A typical client in this phase is a client who does not realize a real business challenge or pain exists in relation to your products and services
   b. Or a client who has no specific aspirations in relation to your products and services

   In this stage, the client would have a problem or need but the client is not aware of it and typically living in the current state not aware of a better way forward.

2. Exploratory & Research Phase
   a. A typical client in this phase is a client who just identified the pain or a possible pain or a possible aspiration in relation to your products and services
   b. Or a client who realized the pain and is still figuring out the impact of the pain or if there is a business case or not
   c. Or a client who realized the pain and passively researching for a potential solution

   At this stage some companies may issue a Request for Information, RFI, or call out vendors informally or formally for presentations. Sometimes clients request budgetary proposals at this stage to test if there is a business case.

3. Assessment Phase

    a. A typical client in this phase is a client who realized the pain and is actively looking for a solution

    b. Or a client who has a preliminary business case or a strong reason why they need a solution and their vision of a solution is not yet concrete.

    c. Or a client who has possibly hacked an interim solution from pieces or parts of the solution but not really sustainable

Typically this client would have a preliminary business case. At this stage, some companies may issue a Request for Information, RFI, or call out vendors informally or formally for presentations. Budgetary proposals are often requested at this stage to test their preliminary business case. Some companies may even issue Requests for Proposals (RFPs).

4. Decision Phase

    a. A typical client in this phase is a client who realized the pain and has a vision of the solution in his mind.

    b. Or a client who is committed to a budget for a solution

    c. Or a client who is committed to a plan, timeline and a budget to execute an aspiration, objective or pain remediation.

Often the vision of the solution is crystallized after the assessment phase. Typically, at this stage, a client will be looking for solutions and would typically issue a Request for Proposal (RFP). But there are always exceptions. It all depends on how bureaucratic your client is and they typically buy.

While I like the above basic categorization of the B2B buying process, it is really hard to capture all the nuances of each organization, and it is important to note that your customer buying process is unique to their organization.

Despite all the attempts to categorize it and make it easier to tackle, the political landscape of the organization you are selling into often outweighs the buying process.

The best way to understand it is to engage the customer and probe about the buying process with different stakeholders in a one-on-one setting where possible.

Although ideally in the buying process, you move forward as time goes by, this is not always the case. Sometimes - hopefully you will not face it - you might regress one or many stages; typically this happens when new stakeholders are suddenly in charge from the client side. What does that mean for you? That means you take one or many steps backward and a lot of the previous work will need to be re-done.

In this case, you might reuse a lot of the work done already; but remember, often people do not value an answer to a problem they do not understand yet. Instead, they need to have their hands held through the problem and then the answer. This hand holding through the problem allows you to build credibility by proving that you know the client business. It also allows you to showcase your work attitude to the new stakeholder first hand to see what it means to work with your company, your team and yourself.

Please note that the client buying process stages are not similar to your sales process stages. Your sales process starts with the first touch point between yourself and the customer, while the buying process exists with you and without you.

When and How to Reflect on Where You Are in the Client Buying Process?

Always reflect on where you are in the client buying process before acting; this needs to be your second awareness! Before any action, understand where you are in the process and ensure your actions are associated with this.

To reflect where you are in the client buying process is to understand at what stage you are at. This is best done with the rest of your team to ensure alignment.

Typically, all you need do is to step back and invest 15-30 minutes, along with the rest of your team, to map where you are in relation to the stages we discussed earlier.

Sometimes you and your team will realize that you do **not** know where you are in the client buying process!

In this situation, it is time to probe the client to understand how they buy and where they are at this stage. This is best done in a one-on-one setting with the most open stakeholder to you or to one of your team members. It is important to have the team member with the best relationship with that stakeholder facilitate this one-on-one discussion and get this information. You can find a list of relevant stakeholders and their role in the buying process at <u>SD2Win.com/TypicalStakeholdersPersonas</u>.

Typically, there are specific milestones within the buying process as you move from one stage to the next. It is important to keep track of the internal client milestones and a week or two before you reach them, ensure you touch base with the client to check how they are doing.

Further, it is always important to Reflect on Where You Are in the Client Buying Process in view of a 'big ask' from the client that would require a significant investment from you.

Bottom Line

Now you know the different stages of the client buying process, why it is important to Reflect on Where You Are in the Client Buying Process, and when and how to do it.

2.3 Secret Concept 3: Peel the Onion

In this chapter, we will again discuss the why, the when, and the how of this concept in the context of solution design.

Why Peel the Onion?

The following concept, Peel the Onion, is also known as the "Five Whys." This is a very powerful concept and it is important to use it to understand your customers and your colleagues better and to help understand better the underlying drivers of the business, technology or a certain situation or results.

Here's a simple example I borrowed to showcase to you the reasoning behind Peeling the Onion.

EXAMPLE

I am late for work (the problem):

1. Why? – My car will not start. (The Real Problem)

2. Why? – The battery is dead.

3. Why? – The alternator is not working.

4. Why? – The alternator belt is broken.

5. Why? – The alternator belt was well beyond its useful service life and was never replaced.

6. Why? – The car was not maintained according to the recommended service schedule. (Root Cause)

As you can see the idea behind peeling the onion is about identifying the root cause of a certain situation.

Why is this important? Because it often helps the client realize what challenges are really affecting the business.

This will help build your credibility and allow you to steer the conversation toward the prioritization of business challenges and what the solution should solve for.

This approach is applicable in your internal discussions with your colleagues or in your external discussions with clients. This is also a good tool to validate your thinking and reasoning before an important meeting or conversation.

When and How to Peel the Onion?

At an Early Stage during your engagement with the client, you want to be questioning everything, you want to make sure you are "walking on solid ground" when you create the solution.

Questioning everything, and many times getting to the root cause of the issue allows you to understand better what can be changed, where you will face resistance to change and what is more or less off limits.

The best thing is to question almost every side of the business as much as you can in an **eloquent** manner.

You want to question everything, but you do **not** want to interrogate the client or your colleagues. As soon as someone feels that they are being interrogated their defense mechanisms will automatically go up, which will ruin the rapport you have just built with them. Make sure you do not come off as if you are judging. If someone has a problem, you are there to help with it and not to criticize.

That's why it is critical to use **Frictionless Transitions** to give reasons to your questions, to clarify your intentions in an eloquent manner, to ensure you defuse the defenses of the person in front of you so you do not come across as an interrogator. You cannot believe how much people will reveal if you just give them the reason and tell them why before they even ask for the reason behind the question. As well, you will come across way more trustworthy. Frictionless Transitions are statements that open the sentence.

For example: "**To ensure that the information I share is more relevant to you,** why do you think this is happening in the first place?."

The first part of the example in bold is the **Frictionless Transition**. I have collated a list of Frictionless Transitions for your use as bonus material. It can be found at: SD2Win.com/ToolsToSteerAwayFromTalkingSolution.

Also, the more effectively you use body language and voice tone, the better you come across as a person seeking help and trying to understand. There are lots of helpful resources about active non-judgmental listening and body language. I added a few links on the topic at the end of the book in the Notes section.

In a sales context, Peeling the Onion works best in a one-on-one setting when you are trying to understand the root cause or even the personal motivators in view of a problem.

In a group setting using this tool is best when it is facilitated by a trusted person, and the problem is well defined. Depending on the complexity of the problem, you might reach the root cause in three **why's**, or you might start creating multiple lanes of **why's**. For example, you have three reasons for the same **why** question, you would have then three lanes and you ask **why's** for each lane. The facilitator's skill is what will help keep the team focused, and stop when the answers to the Why's stop being useful. Typically when the problem is really complex, you will go into multiple lanes of Whys for different reasons; and you might get good insights instead of a root cause.

In a group setting with the client, it is important to lay out the problem and have an open agenda on why you need to understand this problem better. This might flush up political differences between key stakeholders within the client's organization, and you may purposely want to do that to get a better sense of direction. It is important to know when to stop and continue the conversation later with stakeholders on a one-on-one basis if needed.

Another situation where you need to use this tool is when sudden changes or new information or rules pop up out of nowhere. This is when you really need to peel the onion and understand the why behind this new thing. The same exact technique applies - eloquent Frictionless Transitions with active non-judgmental listening.

Bottom Line

Now you know what I mean when I say Peel the Onion and when and how to use it in the context of solution design.

Again, the "secret sauce" here is mainly not to sound like an interrogator while applying this technique. The Frictionless Transitions becomes critical to ensure this does not happen.

This might be counter-intuitive and might sound hard to implement. The beauty of this concept is that it is applicable everywhere, both in your personal life and your professional life. You can experiment and practice in a safe environment such as in your personal life, to get great at it.

2.4 Secret Concept 4: Take Care of Your Blind Spots

In this chapter we will again discuss the what, the why, the how, and the when of this concept in the context of solution design.

First What are Blind Spots and Why they are important?

This is a great quote: "Evaluate what you can see and control, appreciate that you can't see and control the vast majority of what actually happens. And at least once in a while make time to take a step back and think about what you are doing."

I like the previous quote because it summarizes everything about Blind Spots. Let us take it step by step.

Blinds Spots are everything you don't know about the deal you are approaching - business, people involved, business requirements, competitors, etc.

Further, Blind Spots are everything that is uncertain for the deal. Sometimes it is uncertain because the people you are dealing with do not know or because you are not talking to the right people. Other times there is uncertainty because there are other dependencies to resolve that uncertainty, such as an internal or external business review that will resolve these uncertainties in a good way or a bad way for you.

The fact is you will always have Blind Spots, and these are really important because they can change the course of the deal from a good to a really bad position.

Some Blind Spots - for example, competitors - you know you will have, and these are manageable. Others you won't know about until it happens - for example, a change of your sponsor in a deal.

You will always have Blind Spots, and it is really critical to deal with them in the right way.

How to deal with Blind Spots?

When you pre-identify a blind spot, you can manage it. And the way to manage is to **write**; yes, **write** a hypothesis around that blind spot and get it out of your head. The hypothesis could be an assumption about that blind spot or can be a plan for how to deal with that blind spot. The reason why I mention the hypothesis is because the first thing you want to do is to **validate** your **hypothesis**, keep track of it, and iterate it over time. Once a blind spot has been validated, it goes out of the list of Blind Spots - which is a document where you maintain all the Blind Spots.

For example, you might write a hypothesis that includes 'competitor X' in the deal and draft a plan next to the hypothesis to deal with 'competitor X.' Once you get a chance to validate that a competitor is not in the bid, you remove the hypothesis from the list of all Blind Spots.

A similar example could be applied to people, budget, etc., or any other Blind Spot that you think is really important to **acknowledge** that you do not know!

What is important is not to obsess about Blind Spots, although it is important and sometimes critical to uncover some of the known ones. As a rule of thumb, the team is better at focusing on the solution at hand instead, and if anyone has speculations around the Blind Spots, then it is best to **note** them down as comments next to the associated Blind Spot and move forward.

The other Blind Spots you don't know about are outside of your control, and you need to accept that and move forward.

But, what if a Blind Spot that you did not know about is uncovered?

You take that seriously because it means a piece of information popped up that you were not aware of before.

If you are at an Early Stage in your engagement with the client, new information is normal because effectively you are in the learning and discovery mode. This is where you start collecting and uncovering Blind Spots, actively leveraging upon the secret concepts we mentioned before such as "Steer Away from Talking About the Solution" or "Peel the Onion."

When Blind Spots are uncovered late during your engagement with the client, and near to the purchase decision, this is typically a yellow or red flag in your capability to win the deal. Similarly to what you do with an identified blind spot, you draft a hypothesis around it to get it out of your head on the same Blind Spots list; it is often better to do that with the core internal team of your organization. Then actively work to validate the hypothesis by Peeling the Onion externally with the client and creating a course of action as necessary.

You need to keep an active list of Blind Spots throughout the process to be as proactive as you can be when it comes to Blind Spots.

Bottom Line

Now you know what a 'Blind Spot' is and how they relate to designing a Winning Solution, and you know that there will always be Blind Spots, and that is okay.

Dealing with Blind Spots can feel overwhelming sometimes. To manage this, **note/draft** the Blind Spot down as a hypothesis in a managed list, then validate the hypothesis of the most impactful Blind Spots as you progress in the deal. Remember, you cannot plan for everything, but you can hone the skills you need to deal with challenges as they come up.

2.5 Secret Concept 5: Use Simple Solution Narratives!

In this chapter we will again discuss the what, the why, the how, and the when of this concept in the context of solution design.

What are Simple Solution Narratives?

I borrowed the following explanation from Wikipedia: "A narrative is a report of connected events, real or imaginary, presented in a sequence of written or spoken words, or still or moving images, or both." Effectively, it is a story.

So effectively a Narrative or a Story carries certain messages and flows well from one person to another where the key messages of the narrative are not lost.

For a solution, a simple Narrative is a Story you tell about your Solution to different people internally and externally, because generally a multi-million dollar solution often touches many people differently it might carry different messages. For this reason, we want to have a story around the key messages as they apply to different people.

Why are Simple Solution Narratives important?

Stories or narratives more easily flow from one person to another than raw data or abstract information does. Stories or narratives focus on key messages you want to deliver. Good stories also resonate at an emotional level and are more easily remembered than straight facts. And this is what you need because most buying decisions are **emotionally driven not logically driven.** Check the notes section at the end of the book for more resources about emotional buying decisions.

In every conversation you or your team members have with the client, it is best to ensure all messages are consistent. But how do you do that?

Use Narratives or Stories. Because they are easy to understand, they eventually become easy to use and most importantly they stick in a person's mind.

Here's a simplified example of a straight forward fact versus a story:

- **Straight forward fact:** "You said you need to lower costs. Our solution should lower your costs by 15%."
- **Story:** "We have this client, Larry. Larry got a new CFO who ran the numbers and dictated a 10% cost reduction was needed out of the business or heads were going to roll. Larry had a team of 10 people and knew he'd have to fire two or three of them if he didn't find a better

solution. Larry had operations with a large backlog and contracted our services for a solution. Larry installed our solution and, within three months was able to minimize the operations overhead and save 20%, without making any staff members redundant."

Narratives stick because they are easier to remember, which is why some companies may focus a lot on PowerPoint storyboards or animated storyboards when presenting their solutions.

Should you have time to animate the narrative with pictures and construct storyboards, that's good but often selling is not about the slide deck or PowerPoint presentation. When you are having a conversation about a specific topic where your narrative applies, you will not ask the client to wait for a second while you turn on your laptop in order to take your client through your storyboard. That defies the purpose. You want to be on the spot and to the point in time.

When and How to use Simple Solution Narratives?

Simple Solution Narratives are most important toward the end of the sales process when you are (hopefully) closing the deal because you would have already figured out your positioning or the client business case or what value you bring to the client.

It is best to create narratives that focus on the audience of the narrative. So begin by asking yourself: who is the audience for this narrative?

Your audience could be a group of people, a persona or one person. I personally prefer narratives focused on one person. I believe there is potential for a bigger impact when the narrative is personalized to one person's concerns, aspirations, or pains.

If the person you are dealing with is a CEO, then typical concerns of a CEO are often competitiveness, innovation, shareholder value, and market share. This persona of a CEO is generalized and simplified for the purpose of this example. What is important is how to make a story around your solution that addresses the major concerns for the person the narrative is targeting.

This is when you step back, link personal pains to real, validated business problems and aspirations, and tie it back to impactful business outcomes and benefits derived by the implementation of your solution.

The power of having tailored narratives may be negated if different narratives to different people are not adding up together. That's why it is important to look at all narratives together and come up with a theme.

As discussed earlier, you are mainly using narratives in the late stage during the engagement with the client, which means you have already determined your positioning or the client business case or what value you bring to the client.

Now I want to introduce the concept of Solution Theme. A Solution Theme is effectively the bigger narrative around the whole solution. It represents the story you want to tell about the value you bring to the client around the business case, and it ties up the individual narratives together in a way that makes sense.

Ideally, you have one Solution Theme that holds all the narratives together.

This allows you to validate the consistency of the story between the Solution Theme and the different Solution Narratives you want to use for different stakeholders. This will allow client stakeholders to tie the Simple Solution Narratives to the bigger solution theme story and connect the dots consistently among each other.

While you can have a primary solution theme and linked solutions themes, that introduces complexity, and simplicity is what allows narratives to stick. As a rule of thumb, the simpler, the better when it comes to narratives.

Bottom Line

Now you know what Simple Solution Narratives are, why they are really important, and you know when and how to use them.

One final point on narratives, it might not come naturally, and it involves a lot of 'outside in thinking' and putting yourself in the shoes of your audience. I find watching 1-2 minute videos is a good way to learn storytelling. Also, I find *Made to Stick: Why Some Ideas Survive and Others Die* by Chip Heath a good resource on the subject as well as *Building a StoryBrand: Clarify Your Message So Customers Will Listen* by Donald Miller.

2.6 Secret Concept 6: Focus on Building Trust Instead of Selling

In this chapter we will again discuss the why, the how, and the when of this concept in the context of solution design.

Why is Building Trust Instead of Selling very important?

We are selling multi-million dollar solutions. So trust must come first. If you don't have trust with your customer, you lack access to key information because they cannot trust you to provide this information. Without trust, you will lack access to key people because your contacts cannot trust you enough to put you in front of their boss. If you lack trust, your Blind Spots will multiply exponentially in a competitive landscape.

To sum it up in one question: would you spend 10 million dollars on a person you do not trust to deliver what he says will deliver for 10 million dollars?

Typically the answer to this question is always No. Usually, the threshold of spend versus trust varies from one person to another, but it could be as low as one thousand dollars in some cases.

When and How to Build Trust Instead of Selling

When we talk about **trust** as it relates to solution design, we mean confidence in or reliance on some person or quality. When we say **credibility**, we mean reputation impacting one's ability to be believed.

Trust and Credibility impact each other - credibility allows you to establish trust, while trust allows you to grow your credibility.

The faster you build trust, the better and faster you will gain real insight from your customer. So build trust early during your engagement with the customer and build it often.

The first aspect of trust: in a business context, trust is typically specific to a subject matter.

For example, today you trust the electrician to do wiring at your house because he has established credibility as an electrician. However, you would not trust the same electrician to do plumbing or renovations simply because he did a good job with the wiring. You can trust a person in doing one thing in one subject area and not trust the same person to do something else until that same person establishes credibility with you in that other subject area.

If your electrician establishes credibility with you by demonstrating that he has done plumbing work successfully before, then you might end up trusting him with the plumbing. After all, it is easier to work with one person who has demonstrated reliability, trust, and credibility.

You can also earn trust by being a subject matter expert on a specific topic and demonstrating your know-how about that subject matter, and by doing a good job delivering good results to your customer again and again. This will eventually grow your credibility.

The second aspect of trust: Trust is very dynamic in nature.

Going back to our electrician example, when you ask the same electrician to come back and install three new sockets, and then two out of the three sockets are not working, your trust in this electrician erodes because he did not deliver the results that he said he would. Trust of a customer can fluctuate up or down depending on the actions & results of the vendor.

You can definitely build trust with your customer by saying what you do and doing what you say at all times. When it comes to trust and actions associated with trust, I believe this quote by Carlos Ghosn is spot on: "If there are discrepancies between what we profess and how we behave, that will spell disaster."

The third aspect of trust: Trust can be passed along by a person, a reputation or some cultural standards in society the customer can relate to. Here are a few examples:

- Customers can trust the brand you work for, and therefore the trust extends initially to you because you work for that brand.

- Customers can trust a reputation that you have built in the industry - offline or online - and therefore trust is often passed to you when they meet you. Of course, if you do not live up to the reputation, the trust will dissipate.

- Customers can trust a peer or a friend's judgment on a certain subject matter and therefore trust his or her referral or an introduction. Going back to our recent example, if your electrician could not make it, you would probably consider a recommendation from him or her for another electrician; and you may consider a recommendation for a plumber from an electrician you trust because they worked together.

- Customers can trust you because of your title. For example, Chief Technology Officer is trusted as a subject matter expert in Technology, or Head of Payments business is trusted as a subject matter expert in payments or Head of Credit Cards business is trusted as subject matter expert in Credit Cards, etc. Of course, if you do not live up to the expectations of the customer that comes with holding that title, you would lose that trust.

Some of the items we discussed before are outside your control. That is okay. You should not worry about that!

What is in your control are your actions during a customer interaction, and this is where you come prepared so that the customer you are dealing with is happy to introduce you to more senior stakeholders at his company or give a good reference of you to another customer.

Another way to use this element of trust is to ask one of your existing customers to give a reference of you to another customer you are dealing with. That establishes your credibility, but if you do not deliver value to the new customer, your credibility will eventually fade away, and trust will be lost.

When it comes to other aspects of trust, here are a few more examples of how you can earn or build trust:

- Customers can trust you because you appear and sound confident and they can rely on you. You can appear confident by leveraging your body language and voice tone. However, if there is no content behind the appearance of trust, then the trust will dissipate.

- Customers can trust you because you appear similar to them, and you can use mirroring and matching techniques to build better rapport with your customer. Again, business credibility will dissipate if you bring them no added business value.

- Customers can trust people who can relate to them. I

cannot emphasize how important it is to be prepared before every conversation or meeting with your customer:

- **Know your customer.** If you know the role he/she plays in his company, if you know your customer industry, this will help you find relevant topics you can discuss with your customer that he/she deems important and relatable.
- **Find some insights.** Research some small value adds in association with the topics you want to discuss.
- **Prepare some questions.** Early in your engagement with the client identifying mutual topics of interest that are indirectly linked to the deal allows you to build rapport. For example, you could ask: Have you been keeping track of bitcoin? Simple question, it seems generic but may unlock interest in an area that may add value to your deal.

- Customers can trust people who walk the talk. People want to meet reliable people whom they can depend upon, especially in business. Please do not set yourself up for failure by overpromising and under delivering. While this might get you through the conversation under pressure, it is not sustainable.

- Customers can trust people who are open and straight-forward. If you showcase the how and the why, and explain your thought process behind some solution design decisions, also when you admit it was a close call, and you might not have seen all the angles - this creates a lot of trust in my experience. This does not mean revealing all your negotiation cards. It means sharing the why and the how behind some actions.

Building trust is very critical at Early Stage and maintaining trust is important across the entire sales process. It allows you to organically progress throughout the sales cycle as you are referred throughout the business from one stakeholder to another.

Every customer interaction counts. Every interaction is an opportunity to build on or maintain your trust and credibility. Take advantage by planning interactions with people ahead of time and by using some of the techniques we discussed above.

Remember, it is important to pick or tailor techniques that work for your style, that work for you.

Bottom Line

I believe the most important aspect of trust is always to remember that trust is **dynamic**. If you screw up, you lose trust. You've got to maintain trust through actions continuously.

Now you know why it is important to focus on building trust instead of selling, when to build trust and how to build trust.

2.7 Secret Concept 7: Continuously Deliver, Get Feedback, and Integrate

In this chapter we will again discuss the what, the why, the how, and the when of this concept in the context of solution design.

What does it mean to Continuously Deliver, Get Feedback, & Integrate?

I borrowed those concepts from software engineering. In software engineering, it is called Continuous Integrations and Continuous Delivery, so I will use this phrase interchangeably with Continuously Deliver, Get Feedback and Integrate throughout the book. For our software engineer readers, my translation of the processes has been adapted to serve the purpose of this book.

In Software Engineering, Continuous Delivery is the ability to continuously deliver features in an iterative manner rather than bulking a lot of stuff together in one big release.

In a solution design context, continuous delivery is the ability to create a document, collaborate with the team on the document in a short timeframe and then release it early to the audience for which it is intended, in order to get feedback. Releasing early, releasing often, and getting continuous feedback is a very powerful process.

The document you are releasing could be any artifact. For example, a conceptual solution picture, a slide deck for a customer presentation or Simple Solution Narratives or assumptions around the solution that you want to validate.

I know how hard it is to release unfinished work to your intended audience, but it is most important that you focus on the context of the release, and ensure you continuously set the scene by explaining the context of such a release.

As for Continuous Integration, it is one of the enablers for Continuous Delivery. In Software Engineering you have different developers working on different pieces of the software in different repositories. For the software to function properly, all the different pieces of code must come together in a way that does not break the software. That is easier if you are the **only** software developer because you do not need to worry about how your code will work with other engineers' code - you know all the software that you are building. But now imagine you have five developers, ten developers, hundreds of developers, or even thousands working with you on the same software. You could imagine how hundreds of software developers are changing lots of files that need to work together and how easy these changes can be inconsistent and break the software. A similar concept applies to solution design - we will discuss this in a minute.

Continuous integration is the solution to the problem we just discussed, continuous integration ensures that all pieces of software from different engineers work well together - Continuously! In software, this typically includes the following steps: the integration of code, running all the unit test tests, integration tests, system tests, etc. until it reaches a stage where all tests are passed, and everything is functioning properly. This is typically an automated process with a lot of scripts. Different departments or groups of people are maintaining different types of scripts that allow such a high-level of automation. This process does not only ensure the quality of the code, but most importantly ensures the software works well together and serves its purpose.

This is fairly similar in solution design. You do have some checks on your document/artifact before you release it to the client and before you release it to internal stakeholders. The difference in this situation is instead of having software code, you have solution design content, and instead of having automated scripts and test cases you have detailed reviews and discussions around the proposed solution.

But what if we could simplify or automate that?

I believe going through simple checklists against Solution Artifacts before we release these artifacts to clients or internal stakeholders can be very powerful. Checklists should be maintained by relevant stakeholders or departments to ensure the quality of the solution.

For example, let us assume the artifact you are releasing is a preliminary proposal. Then you would check **terms & conditions** against the Legal Checklist created, maintained, and governed by the legal team. In a similar manner, you would check your pricing against a Pricing Checklist typically created, maintained, and governed by a Pricing Function. And it goes on: you would have a Service Operations Checklist, Delivery Checklist, etc. All these checklists are created, maintained, and governed by respective functions.

This will simplify the governance and quality checks of the solution and will typically have higher coverage than a detailed review.

Simple checklists may not cover complex consistency scenarios across the solution, and more detailed reviews might be required. Depending on your stage within the sales process and how much commitment you involve the company with that external artifact, simple checks may be sufficient, or a more thorough review might be required.

Most importantly is to create your own Quality Checklist around your artifacts, specifically around the following questions:

1. Is this artifact aligned with the solution concept? Is it aligned to the Solution Guiding Principles?
2. Is this artifact aligned with the narratives/key messages

the overall solution is supposed to deliver? Or does it break any?

This allows you to continuously integrate different artifacts from different departments, product owners, services owners and ensure that you still have consistency and quality across your solution. You can then run through your Checklists once against your Solution Artifacts and ensure the solution is still consistent. If there are inconsistencies against the checklists, it will be noticeable, then you either fix it, or it is highlighted to the right stakeholders as an exception to be accepted for the "Greater Good of the Overall Solution."

Why is Continuous Delivery, Getting Feedback, and Integrating so important?

Continuous Integration and Continuous Delivery ensure you maximize the quality of your solution and the alignment of your solution to the client's real business challenges, problems or aspirations.

The more often you integrate your solution, the more often you validate or invalidate your solution objectives, the more often you do the checks, get feedback, and execute improvements on your solution.

The more often you deliver your Solution Artifact to a client, the more often you get feedback and the more often you can execute solution improvements.

Further, when done right, your client will be selling your solution internally and they will do some of the heavy lifting because they see themselves as contributors to the creation of the solution.

When and how should you use Continuous Delivery, Get Feedback and Integrate?

Continuous Delivery, Get Feedback and Integrate is a concept that you should carry through your entire deal stage, from Early Stage all the way to winning.

Think of it as a mindset around everything you do in solution design. Ask yourself this question: what is the harm of positioning a Solution Artifact as a draft and getting feedback in order to have a better sense of direction?

Unless it is the last day of submission or the client's expectation is to deliver a binding proposal; usually, there is no harm in positioning your content as **a draft** and getting it out as soon as possible for feedback.

You might tell me, "the first draft is shit! So your solution will be positioned as bad in a customer's mind". I would say, it is often better to under-promise and over-deliver.

You might challenge me, "But you just talked about trust and how trust is so important. I lose my trust if I put a **bad draft** artifact in front of my client." I would tell you to manage your client expectations by explaining to the customer the process you are following. This showcases that your objective is to improve the overall quality ensuring maximum alignment. **Setting the scene** to follow such a process with the customer is important because it allows you to handhold the customer through the process and the deliverables without anchoring your **draft solution submission** as bad; instead, it is part of a well thought out process. That will only augment your credibility.

Use this process all the way through your solution creation. The most important piece on how to use that process is to ensure you continuously set the scene before you deliver a **draft artifact** to anyone.

The challenge with all of those **drafts** that you create is typically version control. This is where using the right collaboration tools and the right organization to win from day one is so important.

To solve the version control challenge, you need a tool that does automatic versioning and makes a rollback easy with full visibility for all contributors. And once you publish, there is a need to have a consistent internal and external publishing tag - this could be a version number, an acronym as a tag, or an acronym plus a version number. And once you get the feedback, if work continues in the internal version (which usually happens) you only need to input the feedback to the internal version once. Ideally, this will notify everyone collaborating on the solution.

When it comes to **integration** and **testing** of Solution Artifacts against Solution Checklists, this is where the challenge is augmented a nudge or two.

At its fundamentals, the actual solution is a set of content documents, i.e. Solution Artifacts that resulted from solution decisions.

Ideally, every team member is following the same solution design guidelines, and their work represented in Solution Artifacts will always align itself to the overall solution and its desired goals.

In reality, that is not the case. Every team member is a human being who can get lost in the details and miss the big picture in view of a narrowed focus.

As part of integrating the work of every team member, you need to:

1. Verify the solution decisions are truly reflected consistently in the content of the solution artifacts.
2. Verify the solution decisions together are not breaking the solution as a whole from multiple feasibility dimensions.
3. Verify the solution artifacts do not break any of the internal quality checks from different departments.

Testing Solution Artifacts against checklists represents an easy tool to achieve the latter.

Another challenge is when and how to write solution tests that service the first two scenarios above, assuming that quality checks by other departments are written and maintained as checklists as described earlier. And when it comes to writing solution tests, should the tests cover 100% of the solution?

Ideally, tests cover 100% of the solution decisions. So, what you need is a Solution Artifact maintaining **Important Solution Decisions**, we will discuss this artifact in more detail later in the book. The team must have such an artifact very accessible when in doubt. When it comes to consistency tests, write questions or simple statements that need to be asked or checked. These consistency tests are then included and maintained in checklists artifacts, and continuously improved upon throughout the process.

Further, this is where some of the agile practices help a lot. For example, daily standups, weekly sprint plans, sprint demos, sprint retrospectives, peer reviews, or pair programming. In our solution design context, these are amazing practices that come to the rescue for maximized solution consistency and quality embedded within the process of solution design.

Definitely, follow similar practices adapted to your timelines. Remember, in a solution design context we have shorter cycles, which means sprints can be shorter or nonexistent. Meanwhile, daily standups always work, and planning sessions always need to take place. Retrospectives are still great, and pair solution design can still happen! What I am trying to say is make it work for your situation.

Bottom Line

Now you know why **Continuous Delivery, Get Feedback and Integrate** is important, and you know when and how to use it.

In summary, use this concept everywhere, follow it as a mindset, and most importantly remember to set the scene with your stakeholders when you use it.

This concept can feel hard to achieve and unnatural at first due to the seemingly overwhelming number of things you need to keep track of. At the same time, it is very practical, and I like to think of it as a new habit - a bit hard at first but the more you use it, the easier, more natural, and automatic it becomes. The sheer benefits it has outweigh the investment and any initial discomfort.

Section Summary

Now you know "The Secret Concepts" that apply across every bid. These concepts are quite powerful because, when applied effectively, they become like habits and increase your chances of winning. For more about habits, you can read the following books: *Atomic Habits: An Easy & Proven Way to Build Good Habits & Break Bad Ones* by James Clear and *The Power of Habit* by Charles Duhigg.

Next, we will look at how to bring all of the above concepts together and use them in the process of solution design during a bid. And how to look at tackling solutions design problems end-to-end. Where do we start? How do we interact with stakeholders? How do we make solution design decisions? How do we keep the team in sync at all times?

In the following section, we introduce The Simple Solution Framework, a system that will answer all the above questions and more.

Section 3: Introducing The Simple Solution Framework

Creating and designing large multi-million dollar B2B solutions to win is often a hard and complex process. This book provides an end-to-end framework to make this process a simple system - easy to think about in a clear mental model, repeatable, scalable, and easy to communicate to colleagues and clients in order to maximize the business impact of your solutions. We are calling this end-to-end system **The Simple Solution Framework**.

Broken solutions don't last. Solution "hit and run" does not work and is just a race to the bottom. What matters are solutions that are relevant to your customer that create a sustainable future for your company and deliver real results to your customers.

Why Do We Need The Simple Solution Framework?

Because there is simply a better way forward that allows us to:

- Focus on the big picture
- Focus on what is important for our client
- Focus on what is important for us
- Have better conversations internally at the right level
- Align better internally towards the same goals
- Qualify 10x Better
- Create solutions aligned to clients' **real** needs, solving **real** problems, and delivering **real** business benefits
- Build credibility with our customers so that they call us for big decisions
- Build solutions that last beyond the people
- Design solutions that are consistently positioned to win.

Following this method will enable you to have the recognition you need internally and externally, which will allow you to get the incentives, bonus, promotions you need for all kinds of personal reasons. Following this method will allow you to achieve continuous growth in this domain. One of the reasons I wrote this book is because I know there is a better way, and I feel it is just wrong not to share it.

3.1 Where Do You Live - in an Ideal World or in Real Life?

Ideal World

Before we introduce The Simple Solution Framework, let us talk about the ideal world of a solution design process. The ideal world will help us visualize how this process will look when different dimensions that influence the solution design process are fixed.

- In an ideal world, we have a clear, well-defined business strategy.

- In an ideal world, we have a clear target market.

- In an ideal world, we have clear business problems identified for the solution to solve for.

- In an ideal world, we have clear business benefits as an outcome of implementing the solution.

- In an ideal world, we have an investment budget aligned with the business case benefits.

- In an ideal world, the key stakeholders in the business are all invested in following the same business strategy with the same priorities; hence personal motivations and agendas of key stakeholders do not interfere with the overall business strategy.

- In an ideal world, the requirements key stakeholders want to achieve are clearly articulated in requirement documents and aligned to the business strategy, problems, and benefits.

- In an ideal world, buyers have a specific, well-defined timeline they go through, and have a very well-defined buying process that is executed accurately with every purchase with no exceptions or deviations.

- In an ideal world, the users eventually using that solution - B2B end customers or internal employees or other parties within the customer ecosystem - have little, or no influence over the strategy or the direction of the solution. They get the solution, adopt it, and use it every day without any friction.

- In an ideal world, everything is fixed, the market is not moving, customers are not changing behaviors, employees are not changing behaviors, expectations from different parties in the ecosystem are not changing, and competitors simply do not exist.

- In an ideal world, steps are linear, the strategy is defined first and gives clarity on the business problems that need to be addressed and what benefits are expected, requirements are defined and are 100% in alignment with the strategy. And the solution is straightforward and addresses the requirements exactly.

I can continue building up this 'ideal world' like this for a while, but I hope you got the point. In practical life though, nothing is ideal; everything is moving all the time.

The Real World

In the real world, everything is dynamic, including strategy, and the entry points to reaching a solution are not always the same:

- In the real world, some people start with strategy, i.e. they define the target market, define the business problem to solve, define business benefits, define and quantify what success looks like, define a list of don'ts, and align all that follows to the strategy.

- In the real world, some people start with an idea and put much more emphasis on action, then they get feedback and derive a target market, business problem, and a business benefit.

- In the real world, some people might start from detailed requirements and then try to link them back to strategy.

- In the real world, some people have an ideal solution in their mind that they want to implement or prove.

- In the real world, some people might start with business problems.

- In the real world, some people might start with business objectives.

- In the real world, some people might start with business benefits or business KPIs (Key Performance Indicators.)

- In the real world, some people might start with personal motivators and derive a strategy based around that.

Further, in the real world, not every customer you engage with is in the same stage within their buying process. For example:

- A client who does not realize a pain exists or has no specific aspirations in relation to your products and services.

- Or a client who has just identified the pain and are passively exploring options.

- Or a client who realized the pain and is still figuring out if there is a business case or not.

- Or a client who realized the pain and has a vision for the solution in his mind.

- Or a client who realized the pain and is actively looking for a solution.

- Or a client who is committed to a plan and a timeline to execute on an aspiration, objective or pain remediation.

- And everything in between!

Every conversation you have with a client is a qualification. The client wants to qualify whether you are a good fit and will add value to the client. At the same time, you qualify, as well, to make sure you don't do the work without the prospect of real business or to ensure you have something relevant to offer.

So how do you decide when to invest your time and energy? What is the limit? When do you have a checkpoint? What is the ideal stage in a buying process to target a client? Is there a right entry point from a solution design perspective?

3.2 Bridging the Gap - Visualising the Situation and Focusing on Impact

The entry point to an engagement with a client could vary significantly from one client to another. Whether it is about where the client is in their buying process, or about how different the real world is from one client to another.

But no matter when you engage with the client and how the client approaches their business in their real world, it is important to have the same level of understanding of the current situation internally within your organization.

Why is this so important?

I go back to an example I gave earlier in the Secret Concepts chapter. Imagine your current location is Location A and you want to go to Location B, except you have no idea where your current Location A is. Despite that, you keep driving around spending fuel and hoping someone will scream Location B so that you stop. To be clear, it is much more efficient if you know where you are, where you want to go and have a map of the destination.

Now imagine the same problem but with a fictional car with two drivers where both can steer left or right, press the gas or the brakes. One driver thinks Location A is in Neighborhood X and the second driver thinks Location A is in Neighborhood Y. How will these two drivers steer the car together to reach Location B if they have a different understanding of Location A? It will be challenging, to say the least!

And what about the passengers in the backseat, i.e. your team or your client in the car next to you? You are trying to guide them to Location B, and he/she needs to trust you while you do not have a clear idea of where they are right now.

That is why it is super important to facilitate a rapid understanding of the current situation. It is important to project that understanding internally to the team. And it is important to project that understanding externally with the client as it builds trust and facilitates deeper understanding in order to design better, more relevant solutions.

To keep it simple, we will define **Requirements** as everything you hear from a client, and that includes: strategy, target market, business pain or challenge, business objectives or aspirations, business benefits, definitions and quantification of what success looks like, lists of do's and don'ts, detailed functional requirements, non-functional requirements, personal motivations, and other factors you may come across. That is assuming

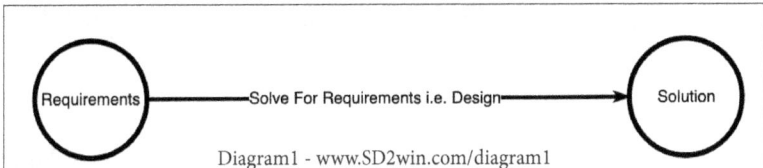
Diagram1 - www.SD2win.com/diagram1

in an ideal perfect world all are covered in one simple category called Requirements. And in its simplest form, the activity of solving for the requirements allows you to arrive to the solution. This is Solution Design as you can see in Diagram1 above.

Another definition for the purpose of this book is what we call **Real Business Benefits.** We use this term when we refer to the many positive business outcomes the client receives after implementing a solution. In this context, Real Business Benefits include growth of revenue, growth of profitability, growth of customers, improved operational efficiency, improved customer satisfaction, improved resilience, reduced risk, innovation, etc. We use the word **real** to stress the need to verify and validate the actuality of the desired outcomes and benefits.

Similarly, let us define **Real Business Problems.** In this book, when we say Real Business Problems we mean business pains or challenges, business objectives or aspirations. The use of the word **problem** in this context is in the abstract nature of the word. To clarify, a "business objective or goal" is something we do not necessarily know how to achieve, and hence it presents a "business problem" to solve. That's why when we refer to Real Business Problems it encapsulates goals, objectives, aspirations as well as pains, challenges or any other thing that the solution is solving for. We use the word **real** to stress the need to verify and validate the actuality of the pain, challenge, objective or aspiration.

In a complex sales process, there are many people involved and often more than one stakeholder. So are the requirements really reflecting the Real Business Benefits to be gained or the Real Business Problems to be solved? Even if they do, are these business problems and business benefits fixed? Can you solve another problem to achieve the desired outcomes? Or to achieve different, bigger benefits?

In other words, why can't we just focus on Real Business Benefits or Real Business Problems instead of focusing on the stated requirements? Why don't we focus on the essence behind the requirements, the **intent**, rather than what is written in the requirements document?

Diagram 2 summarizes what I am trying to say. In this diagram, I am creating a new category within the bigger requirements box and calling that category **The Business**. This category contains the **intent** of the requirements, that is represented in one circle called Real Business Benefits and another circle called Real Business Problems. The balance of the latter two circles is what we are trying to achieve. And the whole box of **Requirements** contains the essence, i.e. **The Business**. And similar to diagram 1, solving for the requirements box - Focusing on its intent: **The Business** - is essentially the activity to design the solution.

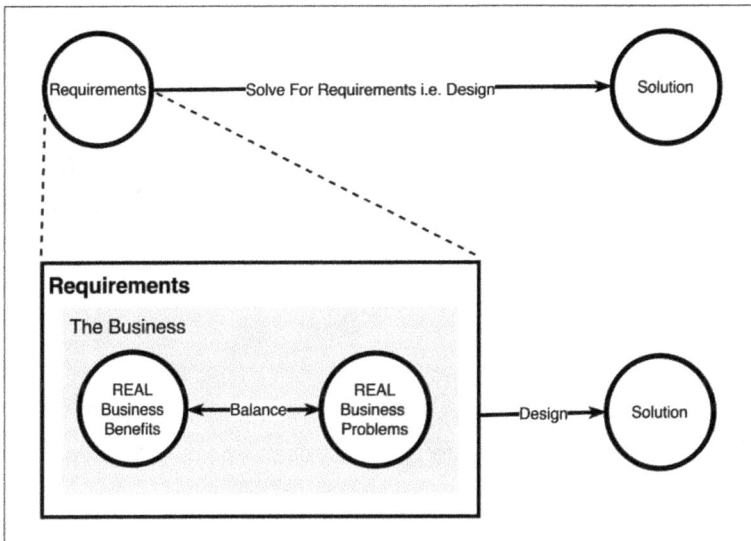

Diagram2 - www.SD2win.com/diagram2

Note: in the above diagram there is only one arrow from the box containing Real Business Benefits and Real Business Problems to design a solution. This is an abstraction, and in reality, there are multiple arrows from each circle. Also, there is feedback from Solution, because every decision made such as Products, Technology or Services often creates certain constraints back on the Real Business Benefits and problems we will touch upon that later in the book. Further, this image is still not complete, and we will work on completing the image as we progress.

Requirements are defined by people, and people have all kinds of biases; therefore, ask yourself, do the requirements reflect the personal opinions of the writers' requirements? Is it a third party consultant or another employee? Or do the requirements address key Stakeholders' Motivations or agendas?

As we discussed earlier, you are dealing with people, human beings, and often multiple stakeholders, which means different Personal Agendas or Group Agendas can impact the requirements. If there is alignment on Group Agenda i.e. Organization Agenda, that's great. But in reality, it is often not the case because Personal Agendas often end up influencing the requirements and the vision of the solution.

The following diagram explains that **Stakeholders** have Real Business Problems in different forms as we defined Real Business Problems earlier, and they have Real Business Benefits as some are focused on outcomes.

The reality is that stakeholders also have motivations, and motivations influence the business problems and benefits. In turn, stakeholder motivations are influenced by both business problems and business benefits.

But how do Stakeholders' Motivations **get influenced by** Business Problems and Business Benefits?

When you uncover a new Business Problem or Business Benefit, or you are able to present a Business Problem and a Business Benefit in a different way, you are helping the client learn something new about their own business - that is impactful and memorable. The client will either have an "Aha" moment or will be surprised positively. This means the client can relate to it. Not only is this a great way to differentiate and build a lot of credibility for you and your company, but this is also an opportunity to showcase a new perspective that can possibly play to his or her personal motivations, hence the influence.

How do Stakeholders' Motivations **influence** business problems and business benefits?

In an ideal world, personal motivations do not impact The Business. The personal motivations are always aligned naturally or organizationally to the business problems, benefits, objectives, and overall strategy. In the real world, sometimes organizational incentive structures of different stakeholders might turn stakeholders' behavior against the bigger compelling business benefit in favor of a benefit that is aligned to their incentives. There is a fine balance to achieve here.

A great way to qualify how big a role personal motivators play in a stakeholder decision is to have a one-on-one conversation with specific stakeholders to get a feel for where those motivators may lie and test for it. There are many tactics to get access to stakeholders or to get stakeholders to open up. There are many writings and books on this topic, one of my favorites is *Just Listen: Discover the Secret to Getting Through to Absolutely Anyone* by Mark Goulston.

Further, understanding the impact of the decision you make in the solution design on personal motivators is a key aspect to be considered and addressed when making solution decisions.

This is a continuous, iterative process. Sometimes you may decide to disregard a personal motivation purposefully, and that is okay.

In the following image, Stakeholders and their Motivations are grouped in a new category called **The People**, and this category is under the same bigger requirements category because The People are creating the **Requirements**. If The People change, the Requirements will often change. So, another critical aspect of the requirements to focus on is The People and how The People influence **The Business** and keep that in check during the solution design process.

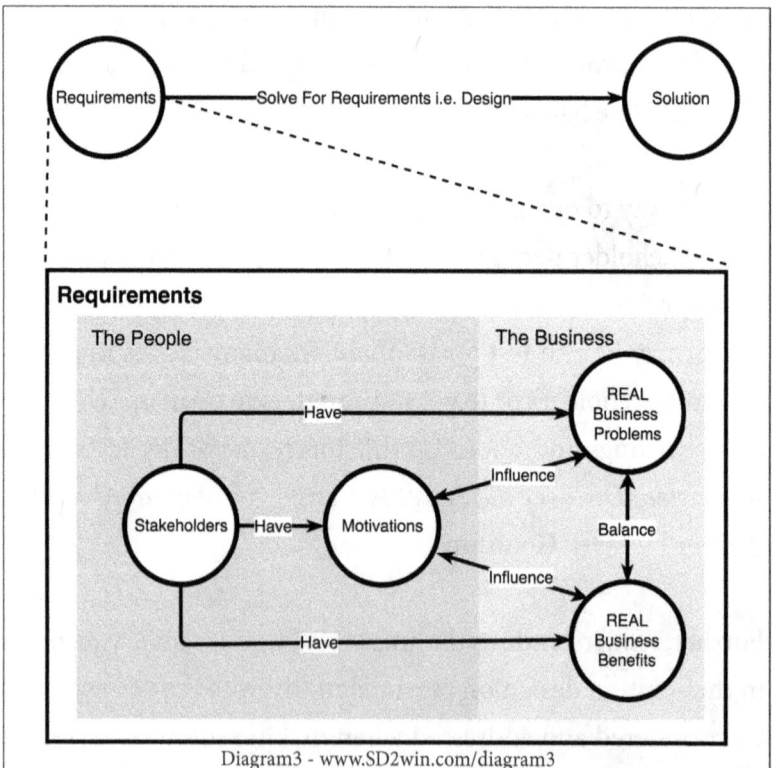

Diagram3 - www.SD2win.com/diagram3

In this way, there is a continuous focus on the intent behind the requirement and that is represented by The People and The Business.

The idea is that the requirements are narrowed to what is important behind the requirement, and The Solution will then solve a prioritized list around the intent behind the requirement first, get feedback early, and continuously iterate.

You might ask, so if I have a requirement document, do I not read it? Do I instead focus mostly on The People and The Business in order to uncover the intent?

When you have a requirement document, great! Read it, but recognize that it is not a "Holy Document." It is written by people, and you should do your own assessment. When you follow the method I describe in this book, you will be able to focus on the intent behind the requirement rather than the requirement itself. The intent behind the requirement is represented by **The People** and **The Business** as defined above, and that's what matters most to win.

This approach will differentiate you from the competition because you will uncover more value by understanding the intent behind the requirement.

Have you ever been in a situation where you realized you could achieve the intent in a different way than what is described in the requirements?

The result of being able to achieve the intent behind the requirement in a different way while maintaining or augmenting the Real Business Benefits often opens up new perspectives. When that happens - and you don't need fancy presentations to make it happen - the client often experiences an "Aha" moment because the new way to achieve the intent opens up even more possibilities. This is high impact, memorable, and very important because it allows you to reconstruct the client's vision of their requirements and locks out competitors in the process.

Note: "Reconstruct the vision of the client of their requirements" is when the client has an idea or drafts what all their requirements are, and then with your guidance realizes that not all of their requirements they have asked for are the most important - some they might not have considered before and some are valid, but not that important.

The difficulty of reconstructing the clients' vision of their requirements usually depends first on **when** you engage with your customer and second on **the depth** of understanding of their business you bring to the table. Both dimensions can help you maximize or minimize your chances to successfully shape or change the vision of key stakeholders of their requirements.

Let us look first at **Engaging Early** with the client.

When you engage with a customer early during the buying process, it is easier to shape the requirements because the customer has not necessarily constructed the requirements yet.

On the one hand, there will be more time to gain access to key Stakeholders, understand their Motivations, and build your influence as you will have more opportunities to gain and build credibility. Also, there will be more time for you to understand the business in depth in order to bring to the client new insights about their business or to get the client to think about their business in a new way.

On the other hand, arriving early in the buying cycle often means your sales cycle will typically be longer with that client. Therefore, there is a need to play your cards well, I mean you must shape the client's vision of the requirements and at the same time not over-invest in solution design upfront when the client is not ready to make a buying decision. This is a fine balance to achieve. There is a need to do just enough solution design and keep the client intrigued throughout a longer cycle until they are ready to buy.

Now let us look at **Engaging Late** with the client.

When you engage with a customer late in their buying process, i.e. official RFP process (Request for Proposal), then your chances to reconstruct their requirements are low, doable but low.

The reason your chances are low is because you typically do not have the necessary access or credibility to influence and change the written requirements. Also, some key people on the client team are already invested in the requirements that they have spent months building, reviewing, and approving. That's why it is a bit of an uphill battle to change the vision of the customer of their requirements at such a late stage, not to mention you may be up against other competition who are trying to gain or maintain influence. It can be especially challenging if your competitors engaged early and helped shape the requirements.

Nonetheless, it is still possible to reconstruct the vision of the client of their requirements at such a late stage in a few ways.

The first way is when you have a deep understanding of the business, and you are able to present their business problems in a new way or identify business problems or benefits they haven't previously thought of. This accelerates the process, builds credibility fast, and gives you the authority to get the right access to stakeholders to shape their vision as well.

The second way is to create a high intensity, high touch, high energy environment with the right stakeholders from the customer's company. This could be a small workshop or project of value to the client. When such an environment is created, the level of engagement and impact are high enough to go deeper into their business and influence a change in their requirements.

The third way is when you have entrenched relationships with some of the key stakeholders and demonstrated credibility in a way the stakeholders believe anything you say, and would stand for it completely. This is rare as it is very difficult to reach this level of believability with new prospective customers, and it is quite challenging to achieve it with an existing customer.

In my career, I have seen deals won when the vendor engages early or late in the client buying process. What typically changes is that the success rate and the chances to win becomes slimmer the later you engage with a customer.

The diagram below represents the chances to win in relation to the time of engagement on the X-axis and the depth of understanding of the client business on the Y-axis. Effectively, the earlier you engage, the better, the higher your chances of success. Your deeper understanding of the client business will compound the effect on your chances to win. I see this diagram as a good, high-level, simple qualification tool that gives us a gauge on the amount of investment and effort to put into a bid.

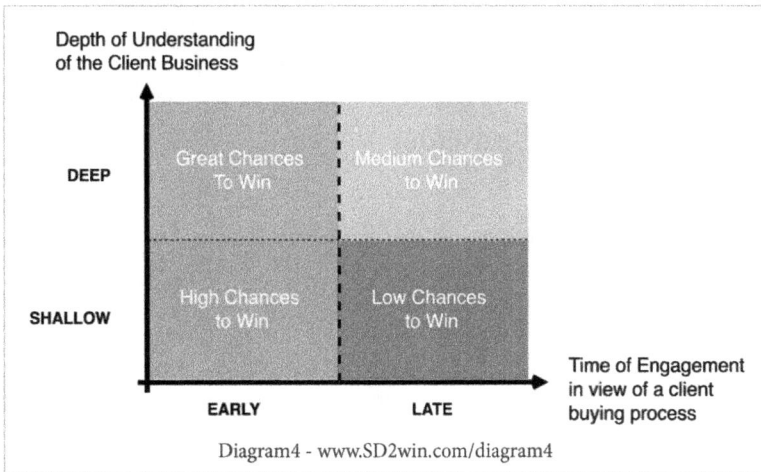

Diagram4 - www.SD2win.com/diagram4

Note: This diagram assumes you generally have relevant products and services to offer to the client in the first place.

In all cases, no matter when you engage with your customer during any stage of their buying process, it is critical you focus on the intent behind the requirement and solve for that first and foremost. This allows you to shift focus and think outside the box of the written requirements in order to bring new insights to your client about their business and maximize your chances to win.

Now we are on the same level of understanding on the following definitions:

- How we define **Requirements** and how we represent the intent behind the requirement, i.e. **The People** and **The Business**
- How we define **The Business** i.e. **Real Business Problems** and **Real Business Benefits**
- How we define **The People** i.e. **Stakeholders** and associated **Motivations**

Now that you know the definitions and you know why the intent behind the requirement is paramount, it is time to discuss how we design a Winning Solution.

3.3 Seeing the Light - Two Major Activities and One Artifact Makes up The Simple Solution Framework

The solution design process is an iterative, incremental, nonlinear process with no single entry point.

You start with a first **Solution Design Iteration**, communicate the first Solution Iteration internally and externally, get feedback, get further information, go deeper with your understanding of the business and the people, and design again a second iteration. In other words, it is really hard to get it right at the first engagement with your customer, and incremental iterations help de-risk the solution for you and your customer.

Note: I use Solution Design Iteration and Solution Iteration interchangeably throughout the book. When I mention Solution Iteration, it is the same thing as Solution Design Iteration.

The most basic Solution Iteration is the first, and the result of this iteration is the first hypothesis of a solution you release. Your first hypothesis of the solution is usually not a complete solution - it is barely your best guess about your understanding of the situation, the desired outcomes, the problems you are trying to solve, the ideal way forward, and the Winning Solution. It might be as small as one of the items listed above, and that is okay!

The result of the first iteration could be as small as one artifact, and as you progress, the number of artifacts increases. Depending on how large the solution and how deep you go, you might end up with hundreds or thousands of Solution Artifacts for really large solutions (think $200+ million.)

Before we progress further, let us define **Solution Artifacts** and **Solution Types** as we will use them a lot throughout the book.

Solution Artifacts

An artifact is a piece of content that you can easily refer back to. It is typically shared internally across the team, which means it must be readable by the solution team no matter what format or document type the artifact is. The artifact could be a text document, a Word document, a PowerPoint file, an Excel file, a Draw.io file, a picture, a piece of code, a configuration file, etc. Most importantly, when it comes to use purposes, an artifact is classified internal, i.e. internal to your company, or external, i.e. external to your customer. External artifacts are typically a group of internal artifacts tailored together to satisfy a message you want to deliver externally to the client, think about how external artifacts need to tie back to Simple Solution Narratives we discussed earlier in Secret Concepts. Now you know what I mean by a Solution Artifact when I refer to it in the following paragraphs.

I will later publish an article that discusses Solution Artifacts in much more detail, showcasing sample artifacts - you can find the article at SD2Win.com/SolutionArtifacts. (when you add your email you will receive the article straight in your inbox once published)

Solution Types

Solution Types such as **back of envelope solution, high-level solution, proposal grade solution,** and **project grade solution** are great categorizations to make it simpler to communicate within the organization what solution you are going for and to get a common understanding around what types of practical artifacts a solution includes or excludes.

I will publish later in 2019 an article that discusses Solution Types in more detail, and how different types of solutions will relate to specific sets of artifacts, I introduce it now because I will refer to it in the next paragraphs and it is important to understand what I mean by Solution Type - you can find the article at SD2Win.com/SolutionTypes.

Going back to our **Solution Iterations**, the more you progress with Solution Iterations, the deeper your understanding of the client stakeholders and business becomes, which results in less uncertainty around the solution, the project, and the overall deal.

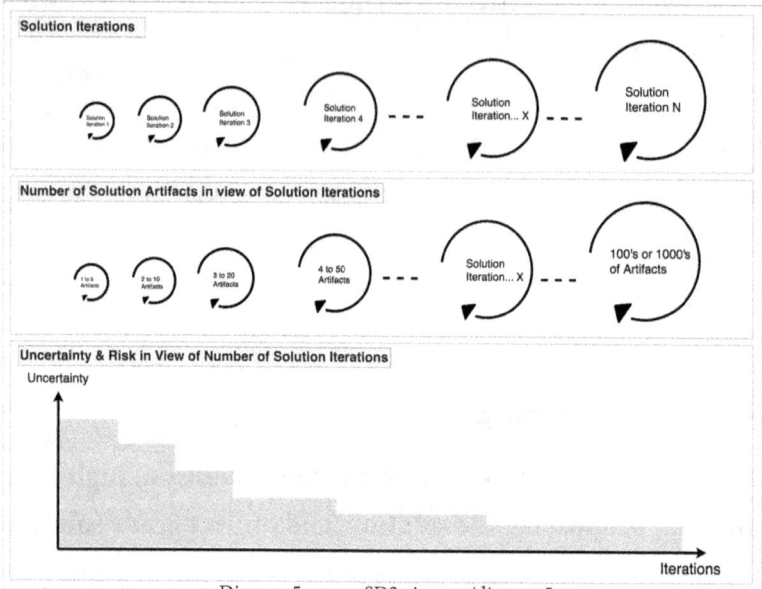

Diagram5 - www.SD2win.com/diagram5

There are many Solution Iterations over the period of the deal as showcased in the image above. There is really no limit to the number of Solution Iterations. Often a Solution Iteration does not result in a complete solution; rather it results in a hypothesis depending on how far you are with your Solution Iteration and when you **exit** a Solution Iteration.

So when do you **exit** a Solution Iteration?

Solution Iteration Exit

You can exit the Solution Iteration at any stage or sub-stage during a Solution Iteration in order to get some feedback, or to ask for information, or to ask for access or to ask some questions, or share an insight or impact, or to share a hypothesis with internal or external stakeholders and get their feedback.

The objective of a **Solution Iteration Exit** is to help you get feedback on your direction, get a deeper understanding, reframe the customer vision of the problem or the solution. All of these objectives can align to help design a better solution to win.

The key measure for a successful client-facing Solution Iteration Exit is to maintain or increase your level of **Empathy and Credibility** with your customer or external stakeholder.

This means you need to **prepare** for an Interaction with Stakeholders to ideally achieve your **objective** from this interaction and increase your level of Empathy and Credibility with your customer.

Now you know **when** to do a Solution Iteration Exit, **what** the objective of a Solution Iteration Exit is, and what the **key measure** of a successful Solution Iteration Exit is.

Going back to the big picture, you are in a Solution Design Iteration, i.e. Solution Iteration. You exit that Solution Iteration and you go for an Interaction with your Stakeholders, then you get feedback, and then you move on to the next Solution Iteration. Check out the following diagram.

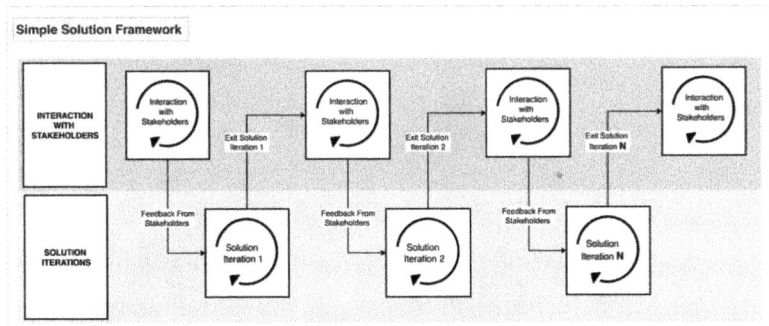

Diagram6 - www.SD2win.com/diagram6

To simplify the solution design process, it has been divided into two major activities:

- First major activity is **Solution Design Iterations**: this is where the solution design work is conducted.
- Second major activity is the **Interactions with Stakeholders**: this activity that brings back athat continuous feedback loop to the solution being designed.

As we conduct both major activities, we generate a lot of information, so we use **Artifact 0** to record information resulting from every Solution Design Iteration or every interaction with a stakeholder. We also use Artifact 0 as a main source of information for our Solution Design Activities, and we update Artifact 0 after every Solution Design Iteration.

Further, we use Artifact 0 as a **dashboard** to access all other Solution Artifacts.

Effectively, Artifact 0 is a central Solution Artifact that will allow you to streamline internal communications, and provide a shared end-to-end live picture of the solution design process, bringing all team members from sales to solution architecture to delivery and operations closer together.

Artifact 0 brings non-customer-facing team members as close to the customer as they can get. The use of Artifact 0 allows you to move fast with your solution team, which in turn will maximize your chances to win.

You may think all of this seems too abstract at this stage! So what are the key activities in a Solution Design Iteration? Can we have a look at Artifact 0 already? And what about this Interaction with Stakeholders? When do we stop iterating? And when do we know we have a Winning Solution?

Section 4: Major Activity 1 - Interaction with Stakeholders

4.1 Three Key Activities to Remember in Every Stakeholder Interaction

You can design amazing solutions on your own without your stakeholders but then who will fund your solution? Who will use your solution? And who will implement and deliver your solution? Who will operate and run your solution day-to-day?

One of the most important stakeholders is your customers who will fund, implement, and use your solution day-to-day. Sometimes this will extend to your customer's customers. In a multi-million dollar B2B solutions context, your primary stakeholders are the ones who will need to say yes to your overall proposition. It is critical to get continuous feedback from your client to maximize your chances of a Winning Solution. You can find details about stakeholders personas typically involved in a B2B deal at SD2Win.com/TypicalStakeholdersPersonas.

Another set of stakeholders is **internal** to your organization or to partner organizations you are working with. These stakeholders are delivery or operations leaders, or both, who may be tasked to deliver or operate your solution depending on your solution scope. Essentially, it is always better if these stakeholders are involved in the solution design workshops - in reality, it is hardly the case - therefore it is critical to loop with your internal stakeholders continuously to ensure continuous alignment with delivery and operations leaders who would be responsible for delivering and operating the solution you are designing.

So we have two types of interactions with stakeholders:
- Interaction with client Stakeholders
- Interaction with internal or partner Stakeholders

Client Stakeholders

What is the objective of an **Interaction with Client Stakeholders?**

Your objective of an **Interaction with Client Stakeholders** is to help you get feedback on your solution direction, gain a deeper understanding of a business problem, or reframe the stakeholder vision of the problem or the solution. All these objectives can align to help design a better solution to win.

Remember, what we discussed earlier "the key measure for successful **Interaction with client stakeholders** is to maintain or increase your level of **Empathy and Credibility** with your customer or stakeholder."

This means you need to **prepare** for an Interaction with Client Stakeholders in order to ideally achieve your **objective** from this interaction and exit the interaction successfully.

Internal or Partner Stakeholders

What is the objective from an **Interaction with Internal or Partner Stakeholders?**

I will start by reciting the following statement I made earlier: Broken Solutions don't last, Solution "hit and run" does not work and is just a race to the bottom. What matters, is solutions that are relevant to your customer that creates a sustainable future for your company and delivers real results to your customers.

Depending on your organization's structure, you might or might not need the necessary internal approvals to go ahead with your binding solution proposal.

In all cases, for sustainable solutions that work, delivery and operations teams must be on-board with your solution, not with the objective to block the solution; instead with the emphasis on "How can we make it work?"

The best way to have this interaction is to have a subject matter expert from delivery and operations embedded in solution design workshops at all times. Nonetheless, that is not always possible as they are executing delivery and operations work.

So how do you begin those interactions and keep them going?

An easy way to interact with internal and partner stakeholders is relevant chat groups for Important Solution Decisions. It is amazing how these asynchronous communications allow you to get continuous feedback on the go to iterate better.

I recommend you always have that interaction going in solution design mode or outside solution design. Information flow is critical and siloed knowledge does not help anyone.

A successful interaction with internal and partner stakeholders often results in minimal surprises, and easier approval flows to get your solution out.

This means you need to **prepare** for an Interaction with Stakeholders to ideally achieve your **objective** from this interaction.

3 Key Activities for a Successful Interaction

For every successful Interaction with your stakeholders, three main activities need to happen during the interaction. You must:

1. **Prove** that you are relevant to the stakeholder(s). Ensure this interaction is not a waste of both your time and your customer's time.

2. **Listen** to your stakeholder with the purpose of true understanding. Why have this interaction in the first place if you don't want to learn about your customer?

3. **Call** your stakeholder **to-Action** by asking for what you want from this interaction. Why set up this interaction if there is no action required from your stakeholder? Why not continue in Solution Design Iteration instead?

Diagram 7 showcases the main activities within an Interaction with Stakeholders.

So the three main activities are **Prove, Listen** and **Call-to-Action**. Which activity you start with out of the three above is effectively a matter of style of both yourself and your stakeholder.

For example, you can start with **Prove, Call-to-Action,** then **Listen**; or you can start with **Listen, Call-to-Action** then **Prove**; or you can start with **Listen**, then **Prove**, go back and forth between **Listen** and **Prove** a few times with the client and then end with a **Call-to-Action**. There is no one right way. It is very situational, and that's why the below diagram representing the interaction is circular with no single entry point and two directions from each activity to the other two activities.

Interaction with Stakeholders

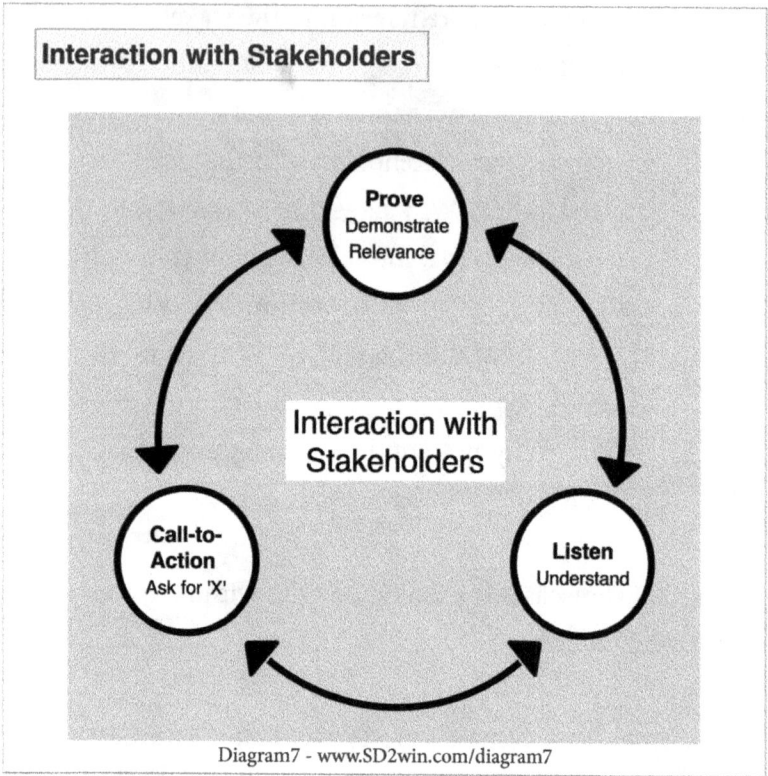

Diagram7 - www.SD2win.com/diagram7

So when do you exit this circular activity during your Interaction with Stakeholders?

Ideally, you exit when you meet the objectives that you have defined prior to the interaction. When the time ends before reaching your objectives, it is okay to ask for more time and continue the conversation over another meeting or call. It is critical to get what you want in order to be able to move to your next Solution Iteration after that interaction.

Let us look at the main activities during an **Interaction with Stakeholders** in more detail.

4.2 Prove You Are relevant

In this context, **Prove** is an activity - it is one of the three main activities when Interacting with Stakeholders as you can see in diagram 7. "Prove" **means** you demonstrate you are relevant to your client stakeholders, always asking yourself this question: Why is this information important for this particular person? Or, why is this information important to a group of people?

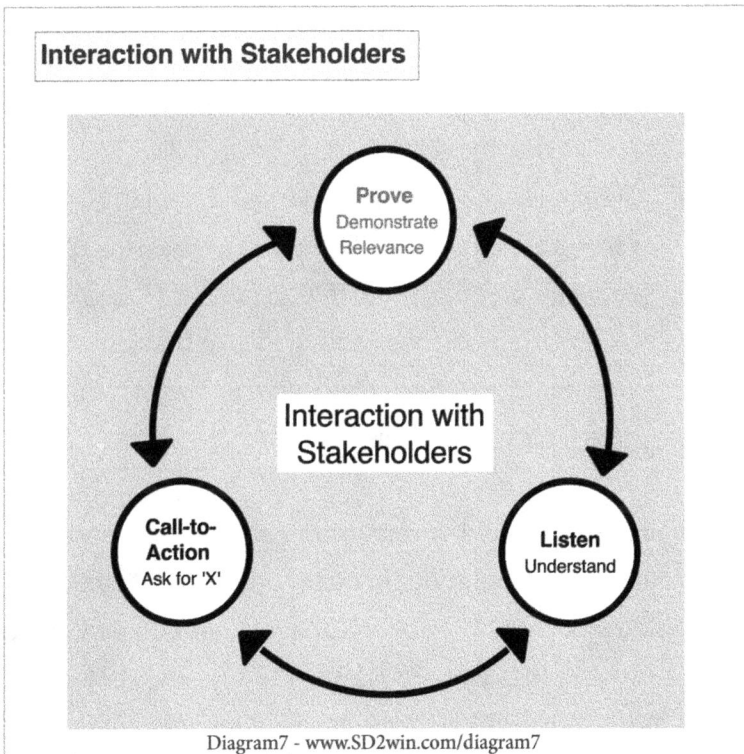

Interaction with Stakeholders

Prove
Demonstrate
Relevance

Interaction with
Stakeholders

Call-to-
Action
Ask for 'X'

Listen
Understand

Diagram7 - www.SD2win.com/diagram7

In the context of **Interactions with External Stakeholders**, every proof is evidence that you are relevant to the customer business or what they are trying to achieve at that point in time. Proving relevance can happen in many different ways:

- Proofs can be quite simple, such as a business card, a title, or knowing people in common. In this situation, the brand and your association with it is the initial proof that you might be relevant to the business problem that the client is facing. This typically happens early in the sales cycle or the buying cycle.
- Proofs can be as simple as sharing a relevant insight and an associated impact that is relevant to the client's business and what they are trying to achieve or solve. This can happen early and continuously as you progress during the sales or the buying cycle.
- Other proofs can be evidence that the solution you are presenting has a feasible business case. This typically happens later in the buying cycle.
- Other proofs can be hard evidence that the solution you are presenting actually works. This typically happens later in the buying cycle.

The challenge in a B2B sales environment is that there are many stakeholders involved; and in reality, these stakeholders are being influenced by other people, peers, and competitors. So despite proving that you are relevant to one stakeholder, you might need to remind the same stakeholder again of your relevance time and time again. This happens because the stakeholder may have simply forgotten about you or because a peer or a competitor has created doubt in his or her mind about your capability to help, or because the stakeholder simply rethought the problem and created doubt in his/her own head.

Proofs are the Why behind your presence in your client's business life. The stronger the Why, the easier it is to remind people of Why they have been dealing with you when they get off track with their thinking about you or your business. The point is: be ready with your proofs and expect you will need to remind your customers of your proofs and use them continuously at different stages.

It is also important to note that being relevant to one stakeholder does not mean that the second stakeholder is fully briefed or that he/she is up to speed and does not need you to demonstrate you are relevant. It is important to know your audience and be ready to prove and demonstrate relevance when required.

Examples of proofs can vary from a **Level 0 Proof**, such as a high-level brand or reputation that demonstrates general relevance to the client, to a **Level 1 Proof**, such as demonstrating an understanding of the customers' industry, their market landscape, and their business, to a **Level 2 Proof**, such as proof of experience with similar problems and solutions, to a **Level 3 Proof** showcasing live proof of experience in similar problems and solutions or an actual subset of the problem and solution at hand.

This 4-level proof system can make it easier for a person to decide what proof is most relevant depending on where they are right now in the sales or buying cycle (Secret Concept 2: Reflect on Where You Are in the Client Buying Process.) This system allows you to use your proofs wisely as you progress further throughout the buying cycle of the client because proofs will always be needed; and you can use them as differentiators or to make it harder for your competitor if you know they will have a hard time with certain levels of proofs.

Following are some examples of Level 0, Level 1, Level 2 and Level 3 proofs.

Examples of **Level 0 Proofs: Proofs of a General Relevance to a Customer's Business** such as:

- Brand
- Business card
- Reputation
- Press release
- Feel free to add your own Level 0 proofs

Examples of **Level 1 Proofs: Proof of Understanding of the Customer, Their Market Landscape, and Their Business** such as:

- Insight and impact statements

- Analyst papers
- Relevant references list or customer names
- Relevant testimonials from:
  - Customers
  - Analysts
  - Or other influential people or organisations in the industry
- Thought leadership papers on market or business problems
- Feel free to add your own Level 1 Proofs

Examples of **Level 2 Proofs: Proof of Experience with Similar Problems or Relevant Solutions** such as:

- Case studies detailed with type of work and their relevance to that specific customer
- Thought leadership papers on problems and solutions relevant to your client
- Snapshots of a Relevant solution or capability - that includes
  - Screenshots or Photos of a solution in action or
  - Process Maps
- Relevant recorded webinars
- Relevant recorded demos
- Relevant self-Service demos
- Relevant self-Service technical documentation (i.e. APIs)
- Relevant self-Service training material
- Profile of Subject Matter Experts (SMEs) who solved a problem relevant to your client

- Dedicated practice to solve a problem relevant to your client
- Detailed workshop describing the "How" in terms of operations and delivery with impact analysis brought from relevant experiences
- And feel free to add your own Level 2 Proofs, this is not an extensive list but this is a good starting point

Examples of **Level 3 Proofs: Live Proof of Experience with Similar Problems** such as:

- Tailored demo of partial solution capability
    - This could be a video call with screen share
    - Or a live workshop
- Showcase relevant Subject Matter Experts capability
    - Again, this could be a video call with screen share
    - Or a live workshop
    - Or a visit to delivery or operations centers
- Small project to deliver for your client
    - This could be a proof of concept of partial solution capability
    - Or a detailed proposition design and feasibility assessment
- Showcase customer references
    - This could be a call with your customers
    - Or a visit to your customer's site
- And feel free to add your own Level 3 proofs, this is by no

means an extensive list.

The 4-Level Proof model is more or less incremental in terms of immediate investment; and as a rule of thumb, you can think of Level 0 proofs as proofs used earlier in the buying cycle while Level 3 proofs are presented during the later stages of the buying cycle.

You may suggest to me that a **brand** or **reputation** is a very high investment to build, so why am I classifying it as a low-investment? In this context, I am not considering the upfront investment you need to build the proof material but rather the investment you need now to use or tailor the necessary proof at a point of time specific to the B2B engagement at hand.

There will always be a need to prove your capability at certain points during the buying cycle, but sometimes the need to prove yourself can be brought forward or pushed back to a later date during the buying cycle. For example, if your brand reputation in the market you are selling into is big, then the proof you will need at an Early Stage will be quite shallow and you can get access to stakeholders much easier or delay the need to offer Level 2 or Level 3 proof until very late during the buying cycle. When you do not have that brand reputation up front, you need to showcase more proofs up front, and you may even need to pull forward these Level 2 and Level 3 proofs.

Depending on how mature you are as a company in a specific

market segment, the need to prove could shift forward or backward in relation to the buying cycle and the interaction timeline with the client. Therefore the level of proof needed could rise to a higher level or drop to a lower level. For example, a company just starting up, or entering a new market, or repositioning itself in the market would require much more proof of capability up front to get access to the right stakeholders in order to have the right conversations and eventually win the business.

In a context of Interactions with **internal** Stakeholders within your organization, the **Prove** activity is typically limited to giving some context about the business pursuit and explaining why this discussion is important to that specific stakeholder.

Internal stakeholders would generally understand that the company is pursuing business, and they are familiar with solution design or sales leaders coming to them to discuss solutions for approval before releasing any binding offer to the client.

Therefore, with Internal Stakeholders, typically context and the why behind the discussion is usually sufficient to **Prove** that you are relevant and move on with the conversation.

4.3 Listen to Understand

In this context, Listen is an activity. It is another one of the main three activities when interacting with stakeholders as you can see in diagram 7.

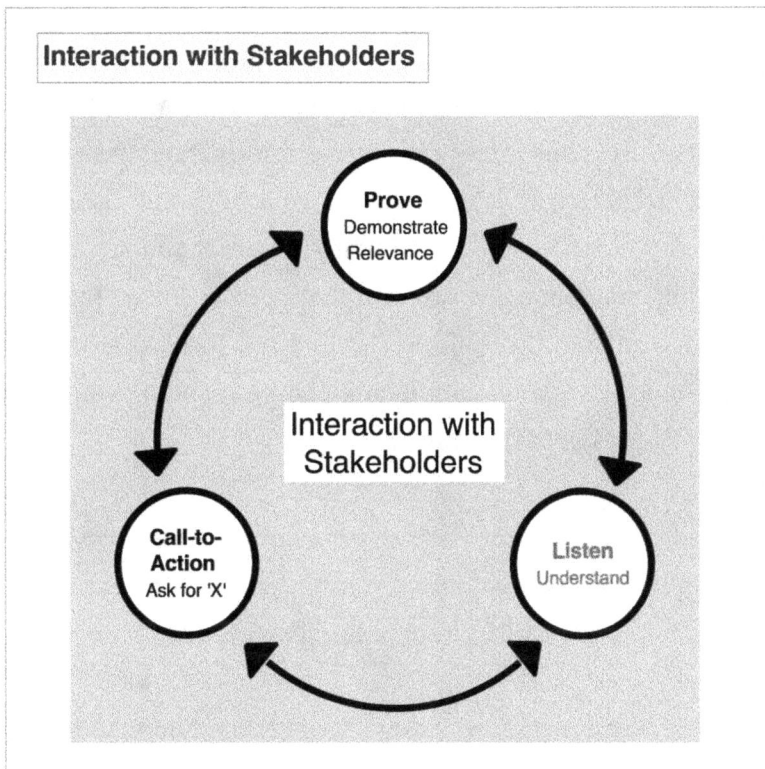

Diagram7 - www.SD2win.com/diagram7

Listening to understand allows you to be more empathetic. This builds trust and respect, enables people to reveal their agendas or emotions, facilitates openness of information sharing, and creates an environment that encourages collaborative problem-solving.

Many books and resources are available on this topic, one of my favourites is *Just Listen: Discover the Secret to Getting Through to Absolutely Anyone* by Mark Goulston. So, I will not go into many details here, instead I will keep it short & simple - following are a few tips:

First, be present, which means giving your full attention without being distracted with your next move or what you want to say next. Remember, people receive information through all senses so there will be cues all over your body and face when you are not really present or faking presence. You are already spending your time anyway with that person, so you might as well pay attention to that person and not to what is in your head; otherwise, you wouldn't need to be spending your time with that person in the first place.

Second, when you are present with full attention, use verbal and nonverbal cues to indicate your presence, such as acknowledgments and body language or facial expressions.

Third, probe for understanding, i.e. Peel the Onion as we referred to it in Secret Concepts. It is much worse to fake understanding than to ask questions to ensure understanding. Again, people can spot that and feel there is something wrong going on.

Fourth, connect the dots with paraphrases to ensure that your understanding is aligned with what the customer is trying to say.

Fifth, get more advanced and use your understanding to reframe a problem in a new way for the customer. Describing the impact of that reframe to gain even more credibility and authority with your customer. You could think of this as a Proof, continuously demonstrating that you are relevant.

In summary, listening to understand involves understanding the meaning behind the sentences, keeping track of the different points in the conversation, and knowing when it is time to rephrase or reframe to ensure understanding. This allows you to build more empathy and credibility with your customer, which in turn will allow you to identify and uncover real areas of concern where you need to take some action during your Solution Design Iterations.

4.4 Call Them to Action

In this context, Call-to-Action is another one of the main three activities when interacting with stakeholders as you can see in diagram 7. A Call-to-Action is important because without a Call-to-Action you often lack focus on the objective or possibly miss the point of the conversation.

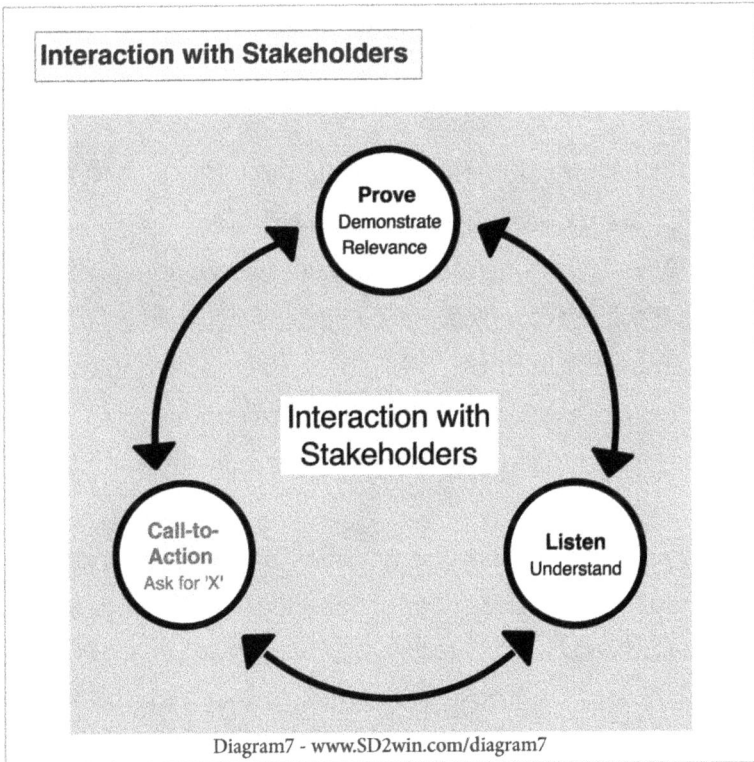

Interaction with Stakeholders

Prove
Demonstrate
Relevance

Interaction with Stakeholders

Call-to-Action
Ask for 'X'

Listen
Understand

Diagram7 - www.SD2win.com/diagram7

A Call-to-Action could be a simple ask for feedback. For example, "Does that make sense?" or it could be a hard ask for business by a certain date.

In diagram 7, under **Call-to-Action**, it reads "Ask for 'X.'" It means, ask for anything that helps qualify, de-risk or progress the solution design. Following is a list of possible asks to relate better to it:

- You can ask for feedback
- Or ask for a buy-in
- Or ask for commitment
- Or ask for time
- Or ask for support (Internal Stakeholders)
- Or ask for access to other stakeholders or subject matter experts
- Or ask for competitive information
- Or ask for other important information
- Or ask for money against a small service or logistics
- Or ask for money against a bigger service
- Or ask for business
- You can ask for anything that helps you progress in your Solution Design and help deliver value to your customer

When preparing for an Interaction with Stakeholders, thinking about the objective of your interaction is critical and designing calls-to-action in alignment with your objectives from this interaction will help you exit this interaction achieving your objectives.

Section 4 Summary - Interaction with Stakeholders

In summary, every Solution Iteration Exit is effectively a conversational Interaction with Stakeholders. And conversations can go in any direction and start from any point. I believe the main activities within a customer interaction could be repeated a few times until you reach common ground and successfully exit an Interaction with Stakeholders. Once you exit with what you need, you can go back and work on your next Solution Iteration.

Interaction with Stakeholders

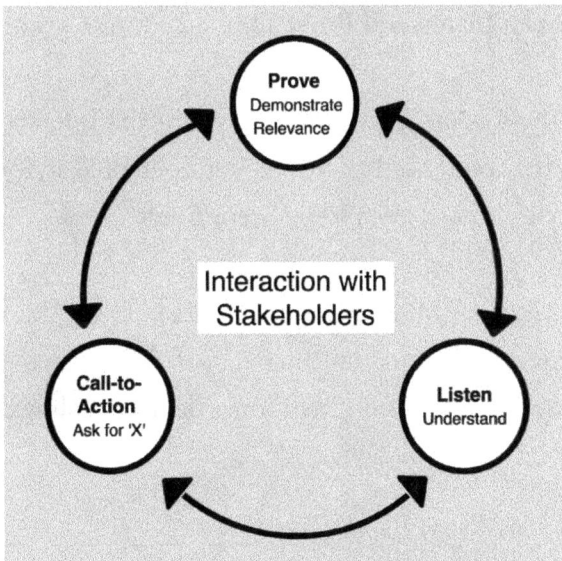

Diagram7 - www.SD2win.com/diagram7

Diagram 7 showcases the main activities within an Interaction with Stakeholders.

Demonstrating relevance is very important because you are spending your time and the customer's time and you must value both. Therefore, being relevant gives you that authority with the customer.

Listening to understand, then demonstrating that understanding allows you to build empathy with the customer, showing that you are thinking from the customer's perspective and not only out of vendor interest.

The back and forth between **Listen** and **Prove** is what will allow you to build empathy and credibility with your customer to "call your customer to-action" and exit the loop or continuously loop between **Listen** and **Prove** to find common ground.

Further, there is no single entry point for the Interaction with Stakeholders, rather it depends on your personal style or stakeholder style and can be tailored accordingly.

Once you exit an Interaction with Stakeholders, the feedback you have received from Stakeholders will allow you to go deeper into your next Solution Iteration. Diagram 6 showcases just that.

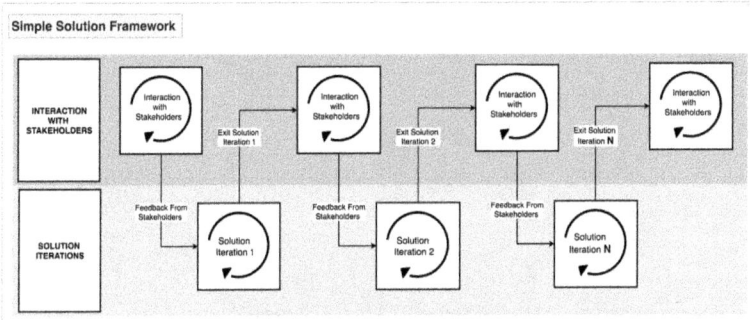

Diagram6 - www.SD2win.com/diagram6

Note: While we anticipate that every Solution Iteration is incremental and cumulative, the next Solution Iteration is typically bigger in size than the prior Solution Iteration. This has not been reflected in this diagram to keep the message focused on the flow.

Finally, it is always important to remember that the key measure for successful Solution Iteration exit is to maintain or increase your level of **Empathy and Credibility** with your customer or stakeholder because that is what ensures you will have the most information and influence, which in turn maximizes your chances to win.

Section 5: Major Activity 2 - Solution Design Iteration

5.1 Three Key Activities to Remember in Every Solution Design Iteration

It is now time to break down the Solution Design Iteration into smaller pieces.

The following image showcases three key activities as part of a Solution Iteration. These are **Understand the Situation, Shape the Solution** and **Make Solution Decisions.**

As you can see in the diagram 8, these are not steps, and each activity influences the two other activities, so balance is important.

Different people have different styles. Some people prefer to start making solution decisions earlier rather than understanding the situation. Then they will validate this hypothesis with feedback toward understanding the solution or shaping the solution.

I recommend starting with Understanding the Situation, followed by Shaping the Solution and then Making Solution Decisions. This is important when there are many team members involved in working on the solution and serves for better communication and alignment. For the same reasons, this is also important during client interactions or internal stakeholders interactions.

The idea is to refer to this structure of activities in a conversation with the team so that everyone is able to follow where you are at any point in time. For example, during a discussion you could simply ask team members:

- Are you trying to **Understand The Situation?**
- Are you **Shaping the Solution?**
- Are you **Making a Solution Decision?**

This will allow you to baseline the conversation and have much more effective conversations.

I want to emphasize again that different people have different styles when it comes to which activity they start with, and that is okay. The idea with this structure of activities is not to stifle creativity with rigid steps; but instead, have each person thinking in their own way. Meanwhile, it is easy to baseline the activities in a group setting, ensuring everyone is contributing to the desired wildly important objective, which is a Winning Solution.

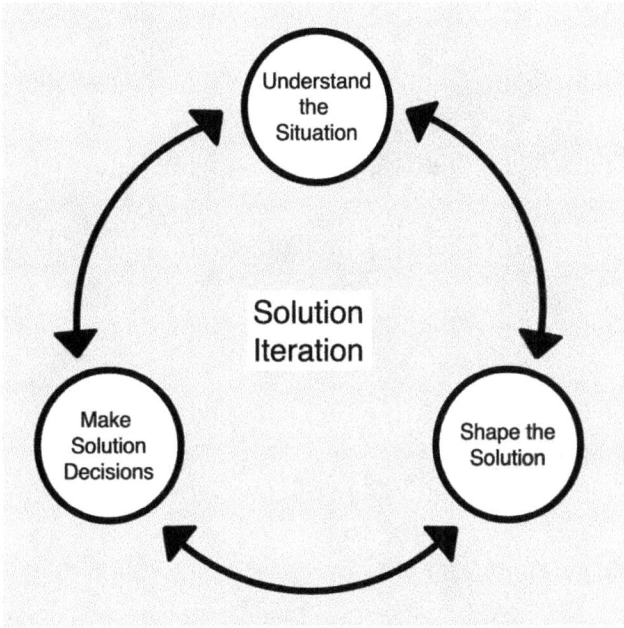

Diagram8 - www.SD2win.com/diagram8

I suggest juggling between two hats while executing Solution Iterations. The first hat is the Client Hat where you design solution capabilities for an "Ideal Way Forward." The second hat is your Vendor Hat to design for The Winning Solution. I will refer back to this concept in the following paragraphs.

5.2 Understand the Situation or Call for Help

The first activity in a Solution Design Iteration is learning and discovery in order to have a better understanding of the situation at hand and have a deeper level of understanding of the problem you are trying to solve for.

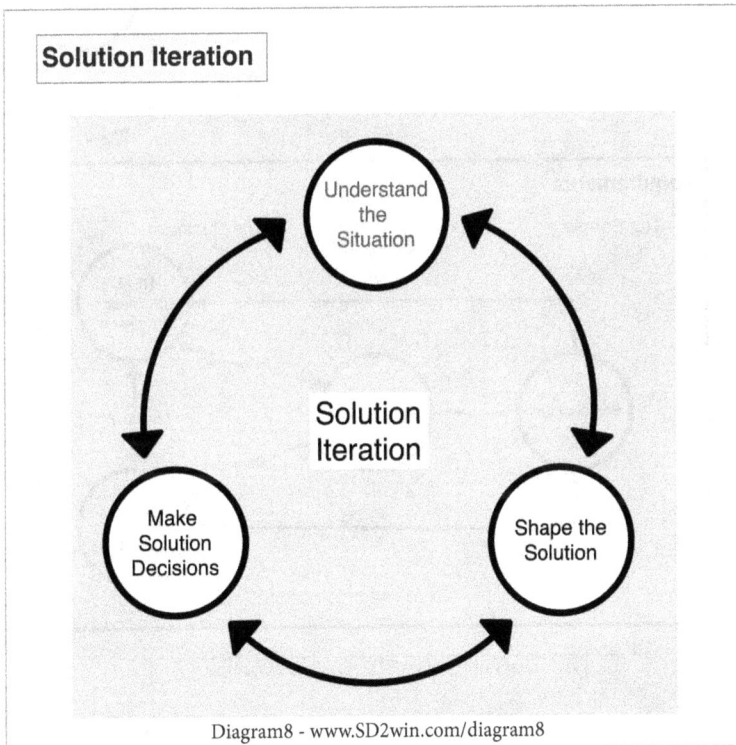

Solution Iteration

Understand the Situation

Solution Iteration

Make Solution Decisions

Shape the Solution

Diagram8 - www.SD2win.com/diagram8

As discussed earlier, focus on the **intent** behind the **Requirements**. Which means:

- Focus on The People, i.e. Stakeholders and associated Motivations
- And focus on The Business, i.e. Real Business Problems and Real Business Benefits

The diagram below showcases how we define the **intent** behind the Requirements as The People and The Business.

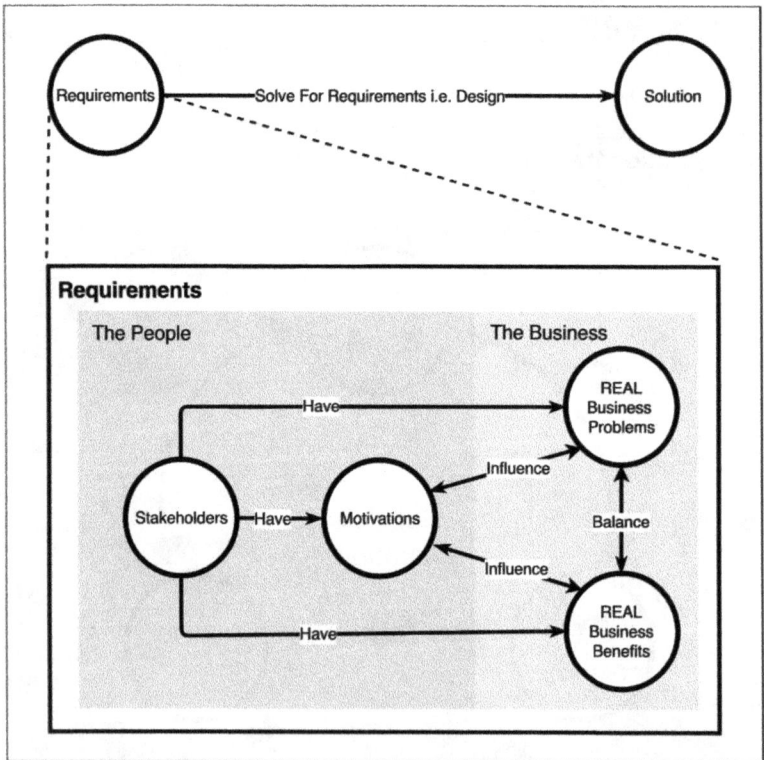

Diagram9 - www.SD2win.com/diagram9

Learning and Discovering The People and The Business is critical to building your understanding of the situation.

The following picture represents an internal artifact that helps to collect the latter information as a hypothesis of your understanding of The People and The Business. We will call it **Artifact 0** and refer back to it in the book as **Artifact 0**. This is a simplified version of **Artifact 0** and will be completed as we draw the full picture in the following chapters in the book.

Effectively, this internal artifact is simply a long list of Stakeholders, their Motivations, their Real Business Benefits, and their Real Business Problems all listed as text in one page and grouped in relevant categories.

In Artifact 0, there are two main categories: The People and The Business.

The People is divided into two groups:

1. **Stakeholders:** In this section, simply list the stakeholders associated with the bid, describe the role/buyer profile they match, and their influence on the decision.
2. **Stakeholders Motivations and key asks:** In this section, simply list what you think people want to achieve personally or professionally or as a company. It is important to highlight deeper personal or professional motivations. Each person can have multiple wants, but it is best to limit it to 3-5 per person.

When we refer to **The Business** we mean:

1. **Real Business Benefits**: In this section simply list what will happen as a benefit if the person or the organization alleviates their business problems or achieves their desired aspirations? What positive changes will they experience as an organization? On a personal level, how might this make the individual feel?

2. **Real Business Problems**: In this section, simply list what problem the solution will solve? Is it a pain, an objective, an aspiration? Is there a root cause of this problem? What are the negative consequences if there is no action? On a personal level, how does this problem make the person feel? Are there any personal negative consequences of no action?

The People and The Business - An Extract of Artifact 0			
The People		**The Business**	
Stakeholders	**Motivations & Key Asks**	**Real Business Benefits**	**Real Business Problem** (Objectives, Aspiration, Pain etc.)
List the stakeholders associated with the bid, describe role/buyer profile they match and their influence on the decision.	List what you think people want to achieve personal or professional or company. It is important to highlight deeper personal or professional motivations. Each person can have multiple wants, but better limit it to 5 max per person.	List what will happen as a benefit if the person or organization alleviate their business problems or get desired aspirations? What positive changes will they experience as an organization? On a personal level, how does this make the person feel?	What problem will the solution solve? Is it a pain, an objective, aspiration? Is there a root cause of this problem? What are the negative consequences if there is no action? On a personal level, how does this problem make the person feel? Any personal negative consequences of no action?
person 1 at a company who... person 2 at a company who... person 3 at a company who... person N ...	person 1 wants to... person 2 wants to... person 3 wants to... person N wants to...	Person 1 To achieve ...	Person 1 Because his problem is ...

Here is a link to the same in google docs: http://bit.ly/SSDFAR0E Feel free to copy, download and use it.

How to use Artifact 0?

Most of the information that needs to be filled in under Artifact 0 can be retrieved from several sources: your direct engagement with the client, the sales leader or any other person internally at your company, or a partner who has directly engaged with the client.

Nonetheless, it is important to do a bit of research around the situation at hand to help you diverge your thinking at an Early Stage and identify key information around The Business, the industry, the company, and, of course, The People. That will help you find relevant correlations, patterns, and differentiators, which improves your credibility and the quality of conversations with your client.

Depending on what type of solution you are aiming for, your research could take as little as 15 to 20 minutes, or up to several hours. You could simply spend 3-5 minutes researching every one of the four categories and add your notes in a separate research artifact or in the same Artifact 0 in a new row. It is incredibly important that you share what you learn with the team, so make sure it is a shared artifact where you can collaborate.

The hypothesis around The People and The Business, along with the result of the research, will help you assess at a high-level what skills, capabilities or experiences will be needed for the solution design, which in turn will help you identify people or organizations internally or externally that can help you with solution design. Ultimately, the people or organizations you identified would be actively participating and invested in solution design. When this is not the situation, it is still good to have access to these people or organizations for on-demand expert support when you need it.

This is a critical assessment that you will revisit continuously with every Solution Iteration as the solution evolves and your understanding of what capabilities would be required also improve over a period of time.

Now you might think that if we uncover all the Stakeholders, all the Motivations, all Real Business Problems, and all Real Business Benefits, we end up with a long list. So how am I helping myself? Am I not just re-inventing the wheel?

The answer is no. You are not reinventing the wheel. When going through this exercise, you deepen your business understanding, and you are able to better empathize with the real customer problems, which allows you to build better credibility with your customer. This often leads to deeper discussions about their business.

Despite ending up with a long list of Stakeholders, Motivations, Real Business Problems, and Real Business Benefits, this long list is useful to shape the requirements and the solution as you will see in the following section.

Note: Solution Iteration Exit
Now a Solution Iteration can simply stop at this stage, i.e. at the Learning and Discovery phase, and then you can engage internally and externally with the client based on your learning and discovery outcome. You can exit a Solution Iteration at any point of time to get necessary feedback. At any point, you may exit with a hypothesis or findings and validate the latter by engaging in conversations with the client. This allows you to share your insights if any, or test your hypothesis with the client. Maybe, by testing your hypothesis, you are able to teach the client something new about their business problems or benefits that he/she did not pick up before or maybe you will learn something new about the client business. Either way, this is a good thing. The key to a successful feedback loop or sharing insight is to be prepared, understand what you want from this engagement with the client (or internally with key stakeholders) that can help you move forward and deeper in your Solution Iteration and solution design

5.3 Shape the Solution or Be Molded by Requirements

Effectively, Understanding the Situation allows you to understand the intent behind the requirements and resulted in **The
Requirements Hypothesis** documented in Artifact 0. Now it is
time to shape the solution.

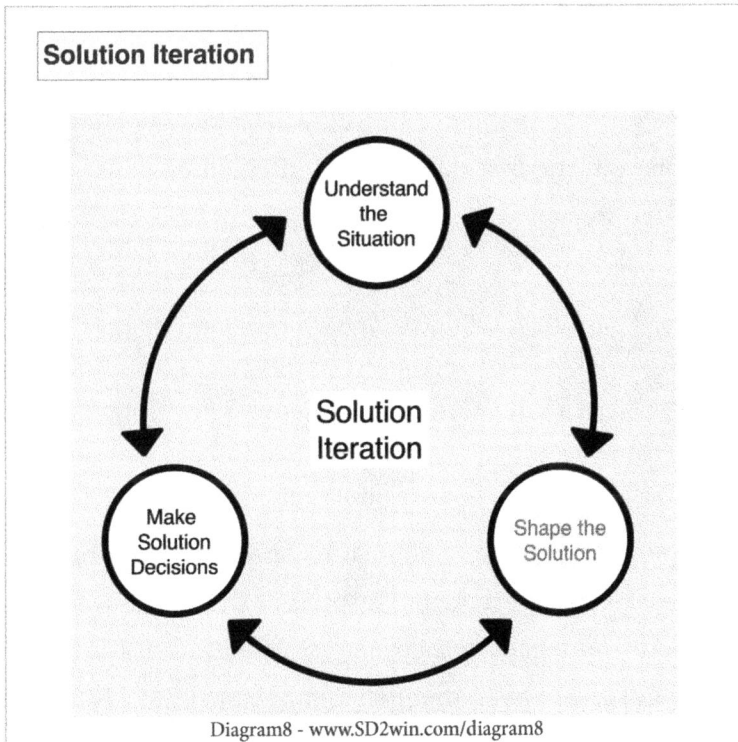

Diagram8 - www.SD2win.com/diagram8

Deciding on priorities of the Requirements Hypothesis will result in a **Reconstruct of the Requirements.** Effectively, we use Artifact 0, i.e. the same artifact, which was a long list of Stakeholders, their Motivations, their Real Business Benefits, and their Real Business Problems, and then we decide priorities on top of the same artifact to help us visualize the key information on one page.

Meanwhile, deciding on priorities is influenced by two other artifacts: the **Solution Guiding Principles** that we want to follow and the **Solution Narratives** we want to tell.

Reconstruct of the Requirements

One of the most important decisions is to decide what problems the solution is solving for, and when you have a big list of requirements, the first step is to prioritize in order to get to a prioritized Reconstruct of the Requirements. So ask yourself:

- Who are the top 3 Stakeholders?
- What are their top 3 Motivations?
- What are the top 3-5 Real Business Problems and Real Business Benefits?

I suggest you wear the Client Hat when you do the prioritization exercise at first. For the purpose of this section, wearing the Client Hat means you do not care about what capabilities you have access to but rather focus on The Business of the client and what capabilities, resources or levels of change the client can take. There are more details about how to approach wearing the Client Hat later in this book.

Effectively, you are reconstructing the requirements in a simple manner. You will put these re-prioritized requirements in front of the client, and you will ask questions about the requirements and feedback about your priorities to deepen your understanding of the business and the people.

Now, depending on where you are during the solution design process, you might need a higher level requirement prioritization or a more detailed exercise - that usually depends on where you are in the client buying cycle and on where you are in your sales cycle.

Essentially, you can add Priority 1, 2, 3, 4 to the requirements as you see fit where Priority 1 represents an MVP (Minimum Viable Product), and priority 4 represents nice to have. Further, using some special tags on requirements such as "Hooks" or "Differentiator" or "Regulatory Compliance" helps you highlight the requirements of significant business impact in order to keep an eye on them during solution design or during communications with your client.

Initially, when you do this prioritization exercise using **Artifact 0**, the requirements and key asks from stakeholders are simple text. I recommend using **hashtags annotation** to add more context to the requirement, for example:

- "Requirement A" #Priority1 #Differentiator #Regulatory-Compliance where "Requirement A" could be a one or two sentence about a feature or other requirement by the client.

- "Requirement B" #Priority3 #CustomerExperience #NFR (Non Functional Requirement)

This annotation is very flexible and adds quite a bit of context to your simple text requirement. Remember, we are doing this exercise on top of major asks i.e. major requirements around stakeholders with Real Business Problems and Real Business Benefits when using Artifact 0.

As for detailed requirements, it is better to hold them in their own tool where you have a lot of drag and drop capabilities to bring requirements forward or backward according to their release priority or according to other dimensions of assessment. Further, it is important to visualize the requirements as much as possible and be able to work on them collaboratively with the team.

Tip: My preferred tool for requirements organization and collaboration is Trello with a lot of Requirements Tags and Pictures, Draw.io for diagrams and Invisionapp for UX/UI of the requirements. If you want to know more about how I use these tools in the context of requirements at SD2Win.com/OrganizedToWin. (The article will be published later in 2019 but when you add your email you will receive the article straight in your inbox once published)

As part of the prioritization exercise, you might start coming up with Solution Guiding Principles or use your **Vendor Differentiators** to influence the priority of requirements because you know you can deliver on some requirements easily while competitors have a hard time doing that.

For example, you could create a guiding principle called "Artificial intelligence First" because you know you have a Vendor Differentiator called "Business Domain Pre-Trained AI (Artificial Intelligence) capability." At the same time, you know the client has a relevant requirement in the same business domain where you have pre-trained your AI tool. Then you could push to prioritize that specific requirement and create narratives about why it is important to bring this requirement forward. It is often better when it is a real win for the client business case and not only a win for you as a vendor.

My suggestion in such scenarios is to use a tag called "#Vendor-Differentiator" next to requirements you think you need to bring forward or you believe you can do better than your competitors.

Note: We reserve "Differentiator" tags usually for client's own differentiators in their market. Of course, you can change the tags as you see fit. "#Vendor-Differentiator" tag is not highlighted to the client, only in an internal view to your organization.

Effectively, in the same requirements prioritization workshop, you are going back and forth rapidly between requirements prioritization, Solution Guiding Principles, and Vendor Differentiators that you could use as part of your Solution Narratives and that is okay. This is why the arrow in the picture above faces both directions.

The result of this exercise is an updated Artifact 0 with focus on priorities, and if you are late in the process, you would update the Detailed Requirements artifact, i.e. Trello board or spreadsheet or any other tool you use to hold the requirements and link it back to Artifact 0 with the associated impact.

Another result of this exercise is an **external** Artifact that showcases the requirements aligned to specific users' journeys in priorities roadmap, 1 to 2 or 3 years or beyond, while highlighting requirements with special tags such as "#Hooks" or "#Differentiator" or "#Regulatory-Compliance" and showcasing where these requirements are in the vision of the roadmap.

At a later stage, when you start making Solution Decisions about what capabilities or technologies your company will offer, what capabilities your partners will offer, and what capabilities you assume the customer will offer, each of these decisions will influence the priorities of the requirements. As mentioned earlier, you might come to some of these capability decisions earlier in the same workshop, and it is okay to make capability decisions early. It is just important to highlight to the team the notion of decisions and that you are making a capability or solution decision. We will discuss the solution and capability decisions later in the book.

In some cases, you might be constrained by technology choices imposed by the customer, it is important to highlight the direct impact of this constraint on the requirement where this is applicable. Which means you will wear your vendor's hat and start prioritizing the requirements again in alignment with the capabilities you have access to as part of your whole solution design.

Reconstructing the Requirements as per the priority decisions is a continuous iterative process in order to reach the right balance for the Winning Solution.

The Reconstruct of the Requirements will effectively become the new requirements hypothesis that you will need to validate. But what about Solution Guiding Principles and how they help us shape the solution?

Solution Guiding Principles

The **Solution Guiding Principles** artifact represents a set of self-imposed solution constraints to help the team make better solution design decisions, ensuring consistency in the way you design solutions. Many experiments showcase how constraints fuel creativity and allow teams to think outside the box to do more within the imposed constraints.

The larger the solution is, the more complex the requirements are, the harder to remember by a big team, and hence requirements become information of high friction. Despite your attempt to simplify and prioritize in one document or in one artifact, sometimes it is still hard to grasp all information at once.

Solution Guiding Principles are shorter, lower friction, easier to remember types of information. Solution Guiding Principles could overarch the whole solution or could be targeted toward a domain, i.e. Engineering, Architecture, Operations, etc., so it is a good practice to have a requirement. When, however, there is a question about a specific solution decision, the team can refer back to Solution Guiding Principles rather than reading all the requirements again, and weigh how their decision measures against the guiding principle.

Solution Guiding Principles are based on the one hand on requirements and on the other hand on your own capabilities, your partners' capabilities or other capabilities you may not have access to yet.

Solution Guiding Principles could be:

- Technical in nature i.e. Minimize Batch Interface
- Domain Specific i.e. regulatory requirements such as data residency in one country or region or other, such as personal data/credit card data to be masked in transit
- Or business i.e. handles 1+ million users.

Essentially, you can identify patterns in the Reconstruct of the Requirements, applicable across the requirements and this could be a Guiding Principle.

Great Solution Guiding Principles are clear and help team members make faster and better solution decisions. Essentially, if a guiding principle brings more ambiguity rather than clarity, then it's better not to have it! Instead, refer back to expressive requirements or expressive self-imposed constraints.

When you wear your vendor's hat, you generally know your differentiators upfront, and you may want to infuse relevant differentiators into Solution Guiding Principles. That is totally fine as long as the team understands where this decision is coming from and the Why behind that decision.

Some of you may even come up with some of the guiding principles up front; before you even prioritize or re-construct the requirements, and that is okay. Different people think differently, and it is a matter of style and experience. It is important to draft these thoughts around the principles and later on test them against the priorities of the requirements.

The reason why we have feedback from Solution Guiding Principles to the Requirements Hypothesis or from the Reconstruct of the Requirements or to Solution Narratives is mainly because coming up with guiding principles may result in new questions, new information or a new perspective on how you think about the requirements or the Solution Narratives you want to tell. It is a continuous balancing act and continuous iterative tests. For example:

- Once you change the guiding principles, how does that impact the requirements or the Solution Narratives?
- Or once you change the requirements, do your new requirements adhere to the Solution Guiding Principles and do they spill over into some of the narratives you want to tell?
- Or once you have new Solution Narratives, how do they impact the Re-construct of the Requirements or the guiding principles?

Solution Narratives

The **Solution Narratives** artifact is all about holding narratives that connect the dots of the requirements with a focus on the People Aspect and how a certain narrative can address the Motivations of the Stakeholders.

A good narrative often connects the dots of a solution decision, to a Real Business Benefit, to a Real Business Problem, and most importantly, to The People, i.e. a Stakeholder and his or her Motivation (or to a group of Stakeholders and their Motivations if applicable.) A good narrative is also connected to a theme as discussed earlier in Secret Concept 5: Use Simple Solution Narratives. Some narratives might be further extended by adding the impact of not having a certain solution decision.

It is often hard to connect the dots of the forward; so you might **not** have narratives at this stage, and you might need to progress with your Solution Iteration and actually make some solution decisions before defining narratives. It is okay to keep it empty! At other times, you might visualize narratives very clearly up front. In that case, the narrative can help guide the solution, and it is good practice to write them down and communicate them early.

Another way to think about narratives is by asking yourself what are the client facing stories that are integral to our solution? And because stories are easier types of information to flow, they serve as another simplified guide toward Solution Decisions.

Constructing Solution Narratives is an act of scenario analysis and design as it connects different dots together; therefore, there is a feedback loop from this analysis to the requirements hypothesis, the Reconstruct of the Requirements, and, of course, the Solution Guiding Principles. Effectively, we are trying to minimize confusion when different team members read supplementary artifacts. For this reason, the feedback loop is a mechanism to ensure consistency of our thinking end-to-end across artifacts.

Artifacts Maintenance

Effectively, all the three artifacts, the **Reconstruct of the Requirements, Solution Guiding Principles** and the **Solution Narratives** serve one purpose of guiding the solution. So why three artifacts?! Why can we not have one single artifact to guide the solution?

I believe three artifacts serving the same purpose increases complexity. Every additional artifact we add will be subject to feedback loops, to continuous updates and maintenance.

The reality is each artifact serves a slightly different purpose and showcases the information from a different point of view.

Solution Narratives is primarily used externally and to help you think more from a stakeholder's perspective. It is a great preparation tool to focus your external messages better and align it to your theme and stakeholders.

Solution Guiding Principles are self-imposed principles to help guide the team when they are in the details of the requirements to make better decisions aligned to the overarching principles of the solution. It acts as a guidance and consistency tool.

The different points of view of the latter two artifacts help you and your team stress test your thinking around the requirements and their priorities from different scenarios and angles.

That is very important in preparation for your Interaction with Stakeholders as this widens your field of vision and allows you to navigate conversations from different angles to further augment your credibility.

Still, how do you maintain these three artifacts effectively? And is there a primary artifact that drives inheritance to the other two artifacts?

My recommendation is to use Artifact 0 as the single reference point to guide the overall solution. And any update to Artifact 0 all team members must be aware of and assess how that reflects on other Artifacts different team members have created.

You can choose differently, but Artifact 0 does hold key asks and major requirements. Further, Artifact 0 holds a placeholder for overarching Solution Guiding Principles. Solution Narratives can always be constructed from major asks, Real Business Problems, and Real Business Problems infused with Solution Guiding Principles.

On a separate note, I recommend you hold the detailed internal artifacts associated with shaping the solution in one document as one artifact, i.e. Shape the Solution Artifact that holds Detailed Requirements, Solution Guiding Principles, and Solution Narratives in the same artifact. This will simplify maintenance as it allows you to view a list of Solution Narratives next to a list of Guiding Principles next to the different lists of all requirements.

Tip: A great tool that allows you to achieve this is Trello. I will publish an article later in 2019 on how to achieve the latter. You can find it at SD2Win.com/OrganizedToWin. (When you add your email you will receive the article straight in your inbox once published.)

Nonetheless, it is good to use Artifact 0 as a dashboard and add links to more detailed artifacts such as Detailed Requirements, Solution Guiding Principles, and Solution Narratives.

Note: These artifacts require significant maintenance and balance against each other and Artifact 0. This means you need bandwidth and resources to create them. Depending on what type of solution (refer to Solution Types definition earlier) you are designing, as well as your solution team resources and capacity, you might end up skipping the construction of these artifacts at Early Stage, i.e. a back of the envelope solution might not require detailed artifacts and Artifact 0 alone would be sufficient.

Bottom Line

Shaping the solution from multiple angles is one of the highest impact exercises you can do to get a better grasp of the business, the people, and eventually to better guide solution decisions ensuring greater consistency, efficiency, and focus on impact. I cannot stress enough how important shaping the requirements is to make better solution decisions. In the below diagram showcase how the different artifacts influence each other in view of the main Solution Design Activities.

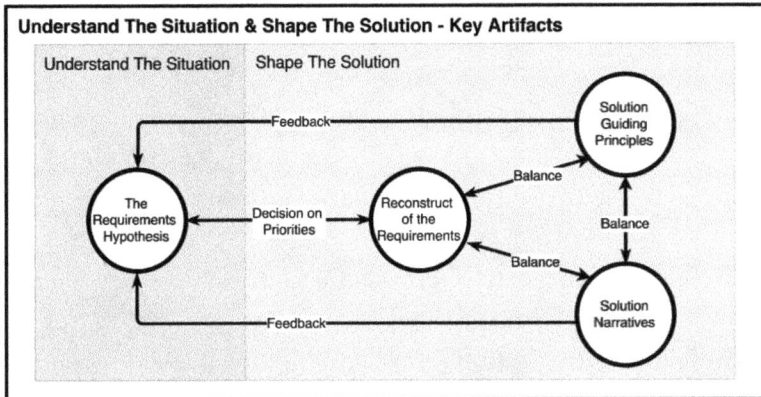

Diagram10 - www.SD2win.com/diagram10

Solution Iteration Exit

Again, you can Exit the Solution Iteration at any stage to get some feedback or share an insight with internal or external stakeholders, i.e. simply exit after decisions on priorities. The key to a successful feedback loop or to sharing insight is to be prepared, understand what you want out of this engagement with the client (or internally with key stakeholders.) This can help you move forward and deeper into your Solution Iteration and solution design.

5.4 Make Great Solution Decisions or Go Home!

Now it is time to make some Solution Decisions. But wait, what are Solution Decisions? And how do we make great solution decisions?

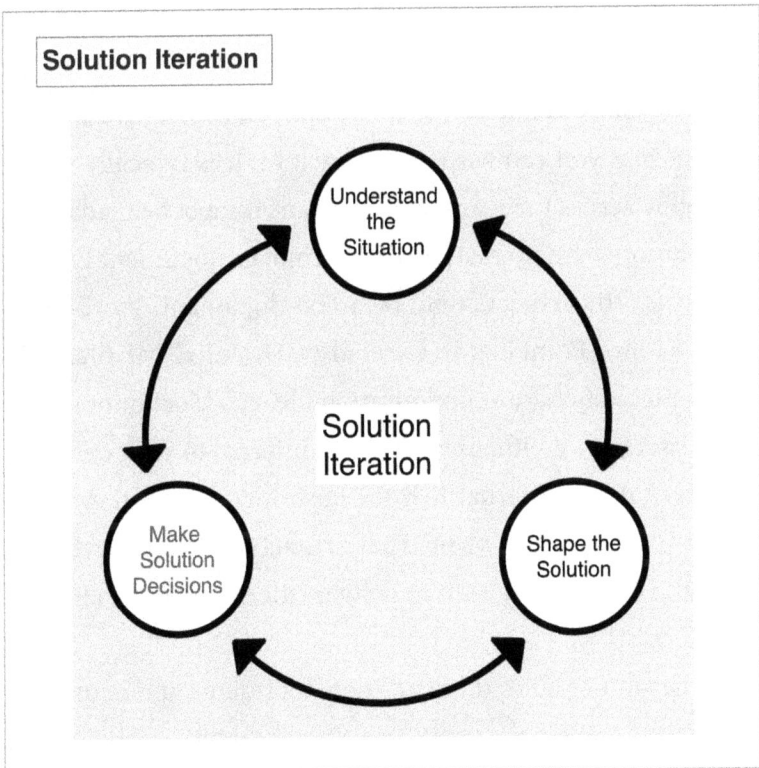

Solution Iteration

Understand the Situation

Solution Iteration

Make Solution Decisions

Shape the Solution

Diagram8 - www.SD2win.com/diagram8

What is a Solution Decision?

A Solution Decision is either a clear choice of open source or commercial technology with its associated delivery and operational model or a specific choice of service with its associated delivery and operational model.

Typically, it is not one decision that makes up the solution, it is many decisions, and each of these decisions gets us closer to an overall solution. The result of solution decisions are represented in Solution Artifacts, and the sum of Solution Artifacts constitute a solution.

Referring back to our earlier definition, an artifact is a piece of content that you can easily refer back to. It is typically shared internally across the team, which means it must be readable by the solution team no matter what format or document type the artifact is. The artifact could be a text document, Word document, a PowerPoint file, an Excel file, a Draw.io XML file, a picture, a piece of code, a configuration file, etc. Most importantly, an artifact's use is either **internal**, i.e. internal to your company, or **external**, i.e. external to your customer. External Artifacts are typically a group of internal artifacts tailored together to satisfy a message you want to deliver externally to the client.

And the sum of all of these artifacts represents and constitutes a solution.

How Do We Make Great Solution Decisions?

Ideal solution decisions maximize the business value while minimizing the risk for your client and yourself. To simplify, a great solution decision needs to make the client business case and your business case. Taking it back to fundamentals, the business case consists of investment, returns, and risks. If risks occur, it negates the returns and breaks the business case. That's why risks are essential to address.

Meanwhile, not all decisions are created equal. Some solution decisions are straightforward decisions, and you could say they have very little impact on the business case, while some decisions require further considerations for different reasons:

- Many options involved with many different consequences
- The complexity of the situation with many interdependencies
- The ambiguity of the situation with many unknowns
- Risks involved can be big
- Stakeholders' Motivations need to be addressed.

Succinctly, the latter decisions would have a high impact on either business case, and to make quality decisions in this regard, it is important to look at having the right setup and having a consistent way to assess the impact of these decisions.

How to Approach High Impact Decisions?

First, start by **Understanding the Situation** as we have described earlier. It is one of the key activities within a Solution Design Iteration. Once you understand the situation in detail, then you are already in better shape to understand the impact of your decisions and make better decisions.

Second, having the right subject matters experts at reach is handy at this stage because it is really hard for one person to understand the impact across the span of different domains in a large multi-million dollar solution. Having subject matter experts at reach could simply mean in the same room, or available over a call or chat group.

Third, setting the scene. Ensure that everyone involved understands that you will be listening to everyone and providing timely feedback on the impact of solution decisions. Some decisions will be close calls and will not please everyone, but your job is to win and maximize positive impact while minimizing risk for your client and yourself. It is always a fine balance to achieve.

Succinctly, It is important to set the scene, listen for timely feedback, assess impact, make decisions, and communicate solution decisions internally to your team and later to the client.

Tip: I find it a great practice to use chat groups such as channels in Slack to discuss the impact, listen to feedback, and to announce important solution decisions. Chat groups present a great collaboration space for solution decisions.

How to Assess High Impact Decisions?

Remember, our focus is to ensure this solution decision while maximizing value and minimizing risk for the client and yourself.

To achieve the latter, we will take a two-step approach:

- First, we will do Preliminary Checks against Artifact 0.
- Second, we will go through an impact analysis around what we call "key solution elements."

Let us have a look in more detail at each.

Preliminary Checks Against Artifact 0

First, engage in preliminary checks to ensure the solution decision is aligned with Artifact 0 and determine if it breaks any key elements of Artifact 0.

This is important, as Artifact 0 represents our core understanding of the situation and holds overarching guiding principles of the solution. If a decision does not align with Artifact 0, it is already a yellow or red flag.

So how do we do Preliminary Checks against key elements Artifact 0?

Simply ask yourself questions about whether or not the decision aligns with the elements as follows:

- Is this decision aligned with the Solution Guiding Principles? Does it break any of the overarching principles? This will help you understand the **Impact on Solution Guiding Principles.** If the answer is yes, it is critical to highlight it and accept it or address it by changing the principle if it is crucial to keep that decision.
- Is this Solution Decision addressing **Real Business Problems** and delivering **Real Business Benefits** on the priorities list associated with the **Reconstruct of The Requirements**? This will help you assess the impact on **The Business.**
- Is this Solution Decision addressing any of the **Motivations** of key Stakeholders? This will help you assess the impact on **The People.**

The result of this preliminary check is to ask yourself if a solution decision is not really aligned to Artifact 0, then why pursue that decision in the first place? A solution decision needs to have strong reasoning behind it in order to continue with it despite the misalignment.

Impact on "Key Solution Elements"

Second, we will go through a more detailed impact analysis around what we call "key solution elements."

The idea is to understand the impact of your decision on key aspects of the solution which may kill your capability to win if you do not get it right. In my experience, while the weight of these key aspects may vary from one solution to another, or you might add one or two other key aspects for specific situations, for technology solutions, these key solution elements are always there, and it is important to check your solution against them.

So what are the "key solution elements"? Why are they important? And how do you assess the impact of a solution decision against these key elements?

Here are the six key solution elements:

- User Experience
- Operations
- Solution Extendibility and Continuous Innovation
- Delivery and Time to Market
- Regulatory Compliance
- Contractual Terms & Conditions.

Remember, ideal solution decisions maximize the business value while minimizing the risk for your client and yourself. This means making the business case for both the client and yourself. The business case has been defined as investments, returns, and risk. Effectively, when you are looking at an assessment of impact, you are looking at investments, returns, and risks.

User Experience

What is the impact of this solution decision on **User Experience** per User Type?

User Experience is extremely important because the friction the user will face is directly related to the adoption rate and actual usage of the solution.

Whether the user of this solution is an internal employee, a client employee, or a consumer, i.e. the client of a client, the same applies. In a high friction experience, users will not be satisfied, and this will create a general feeling of resentment, which in turn will push them to drop using the solution or use a simpler workaround when the opportunity presents itself.

If a solution decision results in a high friction user experience, the risk is a lower adoption rate. This means lost revenue or lower customer satisfaction if the user is a client.

Now, if the users are directly under your control, i.e. employees, in a high friction user experience, you will still face higher user resistance to adopt the new solution, which in turn means higher operational overheads because the change management cost that you will incur will be much higher.

In another situation, you may even increase operational complexity as dissatisfied users may opt-in to create their own small workarounds in order to make their life easier, which in turn creates operational silos and increases operational risk.

That's why User Experience is paramount when choosing any solution for all types of users.

To simplify your decision-making process, a good way to measure User Experience is to use friction and ask yourself, is this solution decision resulting in "high friction," "low friction," or "minimum friction" user experience? Your benchmark is typically a consumer products user experience.

Note: When user experience per user type is part of the Real Business Problems that the solution decision is trying to address, this is just a repetition but an important one.

Ideally, as part of this thinking process, you start building User Experience Journey artifacts, even if it starts as a scribble. Also, it is important to start noting risks in a separate Key Risk and Mitigation Artifact.

Tip: Sketching UX can be simply done on an A4. Take a picture of it and append it to the relevant UX journey on a Trello Board. If you have a tablet and sketch directly, that is even better. If you are familiar with Draw.io or another sketching tool, that is great! Use what works for you. It is important to have the UX journey visualized fast as it helps with having more concrete discussions.

Operations

What is the impact of this solution decision on **Operations?** Does it increase operational complexity? Does it introduce operational risks? Does it increase operational overheads?

This is a big one because it pushes you toward thinking about the target operating model, which party is responsible for what services delivery, and what key points of hands-offs and hand-backs are in the target operating model.

This allows you to construct a responsibility matrix for the target service delivery model as well as map out the key interfaces - interfaces could be process interfaces or technical interfaces.

How does this all relate to the impact of a solution decision on operations?

Typically, the higher the number of parties involved in fulfilling one service, the higher the operational complexity, which in turn will result in higher operational complexity, higher overheads, and higher risks.

An easy way to assess operational complexity is to ask yourself how many parties are involved in the delivery of one business service?

Now, this complexity could be mitigated if all parties have been working together for a while and have proven operational and technical interfaces that work. Or this complexity could be the nature of that process in the industry which in turn makes that operational risk acceptable due to its familiarity and the fact that the industry has known measures to deal with such operational risks.

Another simple way of thinking about operational complexity is to understand the manual work or the manual handshakes or the skill gap introduced by your solution.

The higher the manual handshakes, and the higher the manual work, results in increased operational complexity.

Similarly, if your solution introduces the need for your client to upskill their team or to acquire new skill sets, this will increase operational complexity.

Of course, all of the latter must be viewed in relation to a benchmark, i.e. either current client situation or industry standard, or another relevant benchmark.

Other impacts a solution decision can have on operations is associated with the cost of the new operations. This typically includes:

- Direct service cost to use the service. This may be a license or a maintenance cost or both.
- All manual work and skill required to cover that as part of the operations, including any coordination and management associated with that manual work.

- Impact of manual work back on User Experience, if any.
- Any change management or transformation costs post delivery in order to adopt the service.

A simple way to assess the latter is to calculate the cost associated with each of the points above and assess it in comparison to a benchmark. A benchmark could be the current client situation or industry standard or another relevant benchmark.

Therefore, with any solution decision, it is important to keep track of operational complexity, overheads, and associated operational risk. All three will be summarized by simply looking at the impact on Operations.

In a simplified manner, the question to ask is, what is the impact on Operations? The impact on operations could be high, medium, or low.

When you ask yourself this question, your benchmark is the market and what it can offer today, including possible disruptions. Effectively, you are using your experience or your solution team experience to make a quick assessment. Having the relevant subject matter experts on hand when asking this question is of paramount importance.

Again, in a simple way, you could ask yourself another question: Do business benefits of this decision justify the operational complexity, overheads, and the operational risks?

The answer can be yes, no, or maybe. If your answer on Operational Impact was **high**, while your answer to the second question now is **yes**, then your answer to the first question around Impact on Operation can be changed to "Medium Operational Impact" or "Low Operational Impact."

Note: In exceptional situations, you might know of a competitor that is providing the same business benefits at 10x lower operational overheads and at low operational risk. That's where you might keep the answer to the first question as "High Operational Impact."

Essentially, there are three perspectives: the client situation, what the market can offer, and your own capabilities. The questions above allow you to balance different perspectives in a simple manner while assessing the impact of your solution decision.

Ideally, as part of this thinking process, you start building a Service Operations Model artifact, Service Operations Costs artifact, as well as any associated Operational Risks you add to the Key Risks and Mitigation artifact. Further, you might start sketching a Conceptual Architecture Diagram artifact at a level of users, services, legal entities, and systems.

Solution Extendibility and Continuous Innovation

What is the Impact of this solution decision on **Solution Extendibility and Continuous Innovation?**

While this key element can be counted in operations, I believe it deserves its own dimension because of how big an impact a "vendor lock-in" can have on a client risk's perception.

For example, if the client perceives that they are losing control and there is no potential for innovation without you, this creates a fear in the client, and that often ends up with a risk assessment that is deadly for your solution.

The aim is to show the client how they can innovate with you but also without you.

Also, it is important to show the client how they can keep control over certain aspects of the solution without you. This means the client's decision to go with you does not close or limit their options significantly after the decision and still gives them room for maneuverability.

That's why **Solution Extendibility and Continuous Innovation** is a critical aspect of any decision, despite the occasional assumption that it is part of any solution.

To simplify your decision-making process, there are a few questions you can ask: Is the solution extensible without the need to get back to you as a vendor? Can the client innovate without you? Is there a documented or easy approach that allows the client to do that? I do recommend a yes or no answer to each question.

Ideally, as part of this thinking process, you start building Solution Extendibility and Innovation artifacts and any associated Risks you add to the Key Risks and Mitigation Artifact.

Delivery and Time to Market

What is the Impact of this solution decision on **Delivery**? Does it increase Delivery complexity? Does it introduce Delivery risks? Does it increase delivery overheads? How does all of that impact Time to Market?

There are many aspects that introduce risk or complexity.

First, the higher the number of parties involved in delivering one service or one part of the solution, then the higher the delivery complexity, which in turn will result in higher overheads and higher risks.

This complexity could be mitigated if all parties have been working together for a while and have proven operational interfaces that work. Or this complexity could be the nature of that process in the industry which in turn makes that delivery risk acceptable due to its familiarity and the fact that the industry has known measures to deal with such delivery risks.

Second, the delivery complexity is directly related to the technical complexity associated with the solution. Some of the key drivers around technical complexity include:

- Variety of technology interface types within one solution. While the number of technical interfaces is
  an indicator of complexity, the complexity exponentially increases when the variety of the technology used to speak to other technologies increases,
  i.e. if we have 20 restful API interfaces, it is typically easier to deal with than five interfaces using
  five different technologies that each would have
  their own security and authentication mechanisms.

- The higher number of technical components that you
  have no prior significant technical experience with, but
  you know are necessary to the success of the solution.

- The introduction of emerging technologies to the solution that carries their own risk, i.e. you decided to
  use "The Tangle," a distributed ledger technology, to
  enable low-cost micro-payments.

Of course, the above complexity could be reduced by having
the right resources with the right skill sets to deliver to. And
sometimes you will not be able to avoid such decisions due to
the nature of the problem at hand. Meanwhile, it is important to
assess and understand the impact and the risk, and ensure you
are addressing it internally and externally with stakeholders.

An easy way to assess delivery complexity is to ask yourself the
following questions:

- Does this decision increase the number of parties involved in delivery?
- Does this decision introduce a new type of technical interface?
- Does this decision introduce a new technology that the customer has no significant experience dealing with?
- Does this decision introduce a new technology that we as the vendor have no significant experience dealing with?
- Does this decision introduce the use of emerging technologies that carry their own risks?

Of course, all of these factors must be viewed in relation to a benchmark, i.e. either current client situation or industry standard or another relevant benchmark.

Other impacts a solution decision can make on delivery is associated with the cost of delivery. This typically includes:

- Direct service cost to deliver.
- Indirect cost associated with Time to Market.
- Any change management or transformation costs post-delivery in order to adopt the service.

A simple way to assess the latter is to calculate the cost associated at a high-level for each of the points above and assess it in comparison to a benchmark. A benchmark could be the current client situation or industry standard or another relevant benchmark.

Therefore, with any solution decision, it is important to keep track of delivery complexity, overheads, and associated delivery risk. We will summarize all three by simply looking at the Impact on Delivery and Time to Market.

In a simple manner, the question to ask, is what is the impact on Delivery and Time to Market? The impact could be high, medium or low.

When you ask yourself this question, your benchmark is the market and what it can offer today, including possible disruptions. Effectively, you are using your experience or your solution team experience to make a quick assessment. Having the relevant subject matter experts when asking this question is of paramount importance.

Again, in a simple way, you could ask yourself another question: Do the business benefits of this decision justify the delivery complexity, overheads, and the associated risks?

And the answer can be yes, no or maybe. If your answer on the question of Delivery and Time to Market Impact was **high**, while your answer to the second question now is **yes**, then your answer to the first question around Impact on Delivery can be changed to medium or low.

Note: In exceptional situations, you might know of a competitor who is providing the same business benefits at 10x lower delivery cost and at a low delivery risk. This is where you might keep the answer to the first question as high impact on delivery and time to market.

Essentially, there are three perspectives: the client's situation, what the market can offer, and your own capabilities. These questions allow you to balance different perspectives in a simple manner while assessing the impact of your solution decision.

Ideally, as part of this thinking process, you start building Delivery & Transition Model artifact, Delivery & Transition Costs artifact, as well as any associated Delivery and time to market risks you add to the Key Risk & Mitigation artifact. Further, you might continue sketching a Conceptual Architecture Diagram artifact at a deeper level.

Regulatory Compliance

It is critical to assess solution decisions around regulations applicable to the industry or client you are selling to. In today's world, a few regulations you will come across in relation to data could include:

- GDPR if you are holding personal data
- PCI-DSS if you are holding credit card details to process payments
- HIPAA if you are processing health data
- Local Data Residency regulations if you are holding or processing financial data.

And there could be many more regulations that might be applicable to your solution.

To assess the impact, it is often important to understand the regulations first, then understand the responsibilities incurred by such a regulation.

Typically, as a solution provider, a good practice is to build a shared responsibility matrix where your solution and services responsibility is limited to what you can control versus what the client typically will retain control of.

Depending on your solution and your business risk appetite, you might want to have very limited or no responsibility in this regard. That is okay, but you often still need to hold conversations on this aspect of your solution with the client and make sure you are prepared for that conversation.

A simple way to assess the impact on a solution decision on regulatory compliance is to list the applicable regulations your solution needs to comply with, and then ask, does this decision impact any of the regulations?

Where the answer is yes, you should then ask yourself, is there a known approach to deal with this impact? When the answer is yes, get that documented and ensure it is associated with your decision.

When the answer to the second question is no, generally you are at risk, so you need to ensure you add the risk to the Key Risks and Mitigation Artifact. This can be addressed if the knowledge is at reach within your organization; however, this is hard to address during a bid cycle when the organization lacks the knowledge or capability.

Of course, having the right subject matter experts with the knowledge at reach is indispensable when asking the questions and doing this assessment. If you do not have access to the knowledge, then ensure you have an additional risk to mitigate.

Ideally, as part of this thinking process, you start building the Regulatory Compliance artifact.

Contractual

What is the Impact of this solution decision on **Contractual Terms & Conditions?**

Contractual Terms & Conditions might easily break the solution. You might have some liability terms that you know your company is not willing to accept or the client would not be willing to accept.

For this reason, it is always wise to get Contractual Terms & Conditions (T&Cs) checked early. Get your legal SMEs (Subject Matter Experts) to review and highlight to you any contractual terms that are in the red zone early.

In other times, some legal T&Cs wordings would add additional burden to the solution designed; and to cover it, there would be quite a change to the technical solution as well as to the commercial offer. Again, bringing these forward earlier allows you to take note of them and have a plan to address them in a constructive manner.

Ideally, as part of this thinking process, you start building Contractual Architecture Artifact.

Bottom Line

Effectively, impact-driven decision-making will help you make better, greater solution decisions that will maximize business value and minimize risk.

Note: It is important to highlight that the Key Solution Elements listed above are the foundation, i.e. you might have an additional key solution element that you might add that is specific to your situation. In this case, make sure you add it as part of the assessment. What is important is to assess the impact of your solution against Key Solution Elements.

Solution Artifacts

In the process of assessing the impact of our solution decisions against Key Solution Elements, we touched upon a lot of artifacts that you will build and use as part of your solution, namely:

- Key Risks & Mitigations
- User Experience Journeys
- Conceptual Architecture Diagram
- Service Operations Model
- Service Operations Costs
- Delivery & Transition Model
- Delivery & Transition Costs
- Regulatory Compliance
- Contractual Architecture.

These are, of course, not all the artifacts that you will need and use. We referred previously to other artifacts, and there are many more. The details of the artifacts along with templates, tools, and examples will be published later in 2019 at SD2WIN. com/SolutionArtifacts.

One artifact I would like to highlight is the Key Risks and Mitigation Artifact. We update this artifact in each of the Key Solution Elements because risk spans across all solution dimensions. From a client perspective, the perceived risk can kill any great business case and will hinder a positive decision toward your solution. From an internal perspective to your organization, risks that are not mitigated can break the internal business case and make the deal not viable. Therefore, the ability to have a holistic view of all risks is indispensable because this allows you to ensure you have sufficient mitigations to address significant risks.

Another artifact to mention is the **Client Business Case**. Taking it back to fundamentals, there are three factors: investment, returns, and risks. The work done so far can help you build a preliminary high-level business case. To break it down:

- Investment: This is essentially the Vendor Business Case. This is the cost and price of your services or solution. With every solution decision you make, you get an associated cost and price and you update your vendor business case, which in turn reflects an update on the client business case. Of course, there are other costs or investments associated with the overall project and the client will take that into consideration. To assess other investments of the client, you need to make use of the shared responsibility matrices you have built. Then you either get the right SMEs (Subject Matter Experts) with the right experience to assess a typical cost associated with such responsibility in the client industry or have a discussion with the client to get a better understanding of their costs.
- Returns: This represents the business value acquired by using your services or solution. You have worked already on the Real Business Benefits as part of Artifact 0; now it is time to quantify them and use that work in a business case.

- Risks: You have been capturing risks across all solution dimensions, but do you have sufficient mitigations to address significant risks? What will the impact be of high probability risks on the client business case?

The Client Business Case is a super artifact because it encapsulates a lot of the work across the solution and it helps you focus on the client business. Typically, the better the client business case, the higher your chances to win.

The Client Business Case represents the sum of your solution decisions from another point of view.

Talking about Solution Decisions, you still need to see all your Solution Decisions for what they are - **decisions**. This is why it is ideal to have them all in an **Important Solution Decisions artifact**.

This artifact holds additional information next to every important solution decision. It highlights the impact on key solution elements as well as the results of the preliminary check against Artifact 0.

This artifact will allow you to visualize all solution decisions in one place and track the why behind solution decisions. As you will see next, Artifact 0 will actually hold a placeholder for Important Solution Decisions.

Beyond the business case, these decisions will, in turn, impact your chances to win because some of the decisions will create differentiators and other decisions might create drawbacks. It is also ideal to start drafting an artifact on Differentiators and Competitive Lock-Outs.

But how do you create competitive lock-outs to keep competitors away? And how do you maximize your chances to win? Further, when do you exit for a client interaction to get feedback on your solution decisions?

The latter question will be answered in the following section. Meanwhile, the following question has been answered: how do you make impact driven solution decisions to help you make better decisions? But we did not address how do you approach and communicate solution decisions externally with the client?

I believe in communicating solution decisions to the client in two parts:

- First, is an **Ideal Way Forward** to make high-level abstract decisions wearing the **Client Hat**.
- Second, making **actual solutions decisions** wearing the **Vendor Hat**.

Internally, I believe you can work on a solution hypothesis for an Ideal Way Forward and an actual solution interchangeably at the same time, i.e. changing between Client Hat and Vendor

Hat. And it is often easier to build a hypothesis of a solution wearing your vendor's hat, making actual solution decisions and then going back to an ideal way forward.

Meanwhile, when interacting with the client, I strongly recommend always starting with an **Ideal Way Forward** discussion and then bridging it toward an actual solution discussion. But why should you do that? And how do you wear a Client Hat?

Ideal Way Forward and Abstract Solution

When designing solutions for an Ideal Way Forward, you wear a Client Hat and make abstract solution decisions, which in turn will result in an abstract solution.

But what does it mean to wear a Client Hat? Or make **abstract** solution decisions? Or have an abstract solution? And why do you need to do that?

Wearing a Client Hat

Wearing a Client Hat does not mean solving for all the requirements the client said they wanted; rather, it means to think of the situation as if you were a stakeholder in the client business who is deeply invested in the success of that business as a whole and not only one department.

This requires a deep understanding of the client business, the client market, and a deep understanding of the client's existing capabilities on the one hand; while having a great understanding of the solutions market and what it can offer to help the client on the other hand.

This approach will allow you to emphasize with your client, demonstrate industry knowledge, and have relevant business and solution conversations in view of the actual client business. And that, in turn, will help you build authority with the client during client interactions.

The idea is to be as neutral as possible toward your capabilities while wearing the Client Hat. Nonetheless, your capabilities are a part of the solutions market, so realistically you cannot exclude them.

Being neutral allows you to paint a real picture of an ideal way forward. This, in turn, will help you uncover your weaknesses early vis-a-vis the ideal way forward. Therefore it allows you and your internal stakeholders to make better-informed solution decisions to address your weaknesses or capitalize on strengths or make better deal qualification decisions.

Abstract Decisions
Ideal Way Forward decisions are abstract in nature and do not point to specific technologies. This does not mean you could just name capabilities out of thin air; you need to know that real technologies or service providers exist behind the capabilities decisions you make.

For example, an abstract decision could be to use a NoSQL database-managed service for that specific business problem while an actual Solution Decision would be using MongoDB as a database hosted with cloud-managed services on Amazon. On a similar level, another abstract decision example could be to use a memory-heavy IaaS private cloud service while the actual Solution Decision is Google Cloud High-CPU machines services. Another example would be using a cloud Human Resource Management Software, and the actual solution decision is using Workday or Zenefits.

There are many levels of abstraction as you see in the examples above, and the right level of abstraction is at a capability level where you can have a great conversation with the client. Yes, you could say an abstraction level at the level of serverless technology is different from business software, and this is where you need to gauge and tailor in accordance with your audience.

An Ideal Way Forward, with its abstract nature, allows both yourself and the client to be more open in your conversation because you both are not talking about the technology you are offering. Instead, you may be talking about an abstract that directly relates to that technology, and that is okay. It is still a neutral space where changes in positioning are allowed and what you say, or the client says, is not an opinion directly associated with your technology. This space of maneuverability allows you to get the concerns up front in a low-defensibility environment and position better when you introduce your capability.

Also, this means it is a great place to introduce competitive lock-outs in an abstract manner. For example, introduce a quality standard or capabilities delivered in a certain way that you know your competitors have a hard time meeting. Once you add what you think is a new competitive lock-out, you update the Differentiators & Competitive Lock-Outs artifact.

Further, having an Ideal Way Forward allows the client to come up with the right answer with you rather than handing in the answer upfront to the client. In my personal experience, if you give a straight answer to the client without getting the client to walk through the process and the analysis behind a decision, the answer is often undervalued and ignored. This might be controversial, and I believe it depends on the client style, your level of empathy, and the credibility you have with the client. Nonetheless, I believe in generalizing this approach of walking the client through to get to the answer and creating an exception for exceptional clients who really understand all the details and just want the answer.

Essentially, having an Ideal Way Forward has great benefits; it maximizes your chances to win or to understand your gaps better and qualify out.

So do you need to consider the same impact on abstract solution decisions in the same way you consider the decision impact for actual solution decisions?

Yes, that does not change. That's why internally you might be actually working on a solution decision first then abstract it for a first level communication with the client about the solution.

Therefore, with every abstract solution decision you make, it is important to have the right people with the right experiences and backgrounds to understand the ripple impact of the decision better and assess what the right balance could be.

Abstract Solution
So what is an Abstract Solution?

Just like a solution, an Abstract Solution is a sum of Abstract Decisions that make up a solution. This results in Abstracted Solution Artifacts without a vendor or a specific service provider or brand name behind a decision. Effectively, you will create an Abstracted Solution Decisions Artifact, which is simply the sum of all abstract decisions. The same artifact can be turned into a High-Level Abstract Services Context Diagram artifact and a High-Level Abstract System Context Diagram artifact and many other Solution Artifacts to come.

Should you communicate an abstract solution out to the client and then communicate the actual solution? And what is the impact on having an Abstract Solution communicated before the actual solution?

Once you make an abstract decision, that abstract solution result acts as a constraint for your actual solution choice. So while it can stand on its own as an Abstract Solution, it is not really a solution, it is just a constraint that you look back at when you make actual solution decisions. Because you are introducing that constraint with the client, ideally it is aligned to a solution decision before-hand, and you know you have a capability associated with it.

The Winning Solution

Typically, a Winning Solution matches the client business case, has an acceptable risk profile by the client, addresses key Motivations of the client's Stakeholders, and is supported by delivery and operations teams.

When you follow The Simple Solution Framework represented by the picture below, the focus is on building trust and authority with the client. You achieve that by iterating many times over the solution, getting feedback continuously and often with your stakeholders. The solution is not a surprise solution to the client; the client is invested in the solution upfront because you probed the client to address the concerns. Therefore, the framework guides you towards minimizing your risk and the client risk and finally towards a Winning Solution.

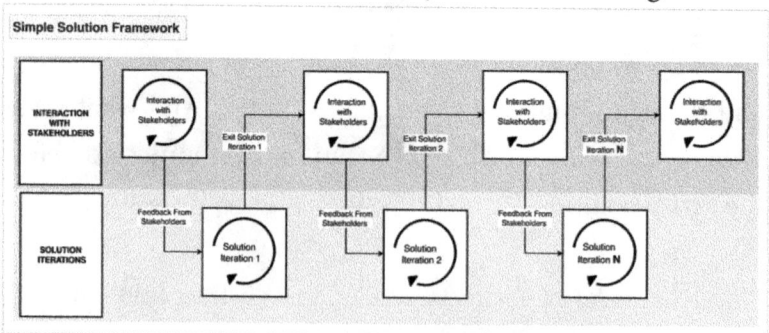

Diagram6 - www.SD2win.com/diagram6

The Winning Solution is effectively the result of all your actual solution decisions over many Solution Iterations within the timeframe of the bid.

The catch is that you have a lot of artifacts to manage and organize as part of solution design, so how do you keep a focus on what is important at all times?

The reality is that we are living in a very fast-paced environment, and in the above structure, the method, the different backgrounds on a team, and the incremental number of artifacts can hinder communications significantly.

Moving fast requires great communications!

To ensure everybody is moving fast along with you, even if they join in halfway through, you need robust, simple artifacts that maximize information flow across teams and keep a focus on what is important.

That's where the concept of Artifact 0 comes in. The idea of this artifact is to have a centralized view of what is important, a dashboard that allows you access to all other artifacts, a representation of the why behind solution decisions, and a place to always go back to as a guide for all the team.

I have shared with you earlier an extract of Artifact 0 during the Solution Iteration activity Understand The Situation, and I have asked you to use it again to reconstruct the requirements during Solution Iteration activity Shape The Solution. Now I ask you to use the same Artifact 0 again when **making Solution Decisions.**

Yes, every solution decision you make for an Ideal Way Forward or for the Winning Solution you register in Artifact 0 and you add the why behind that decision in simple text. Here's a link to Artifact 0: http://bit.ly/SSDFAR0

Artifact 0 Link: http://bit.ly/SSDFAR0

The reason this artifact is filled in simple texts is to maximize the usability of this artifact and minimize friction.

In their simplest forms, all artifacts can be simplified to simple text sentences, i.e. decisions, and we can continuously make artifacts more representative and more visual as we progress in Solution Iteration.

So can you use diagrams or pictures within this artifact?

Yes, you can! And I am all for that. That's where this Artifact 0 turns into a **dashboard** that guides you toward all your Solution Artifacts from a single view by simply adding hyperlinks to more representative artifacts.

Meanwhile, Artifact 0 must continuously hold minimal vital information in simple text annotation to have a very good understanding of the solution and the why behind it in a single view. Strive for that in all your actions.

So how do you fill the artifact in the context of the two major activities, namely Solution Iterations and Interaction with Stakeholders?

Despite the fact that you see Artifact 0 linearly, and you read it from left to right, when it comes to activities the idea is to focus on Solution Iteration key activities as well as Interaction with Stakeholders key activities, and Artifact 0 can be filled from **any entry point** depending on what key activity you start with.

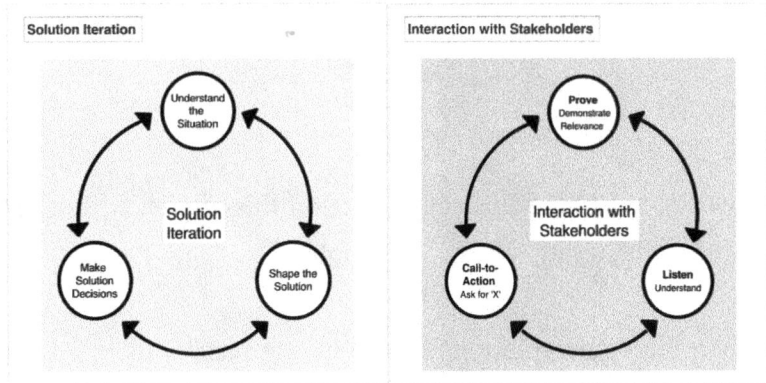

I recommend starting from understanding the situation and then showcasing the output on Artifact 0, shaping the solution and then showcasing the result on Artifact 0, and finally making solution decisions and showcasing the result in Artifact 0. Therefore, Artifact 0 gets updated with every Solution Iteration.

This artifact is also updated every time you interact with a stakeholder and get some feedback.

The following illustration demonstrates that there is an influence of The People and The Business on Solution Decisions, and there is an influence from actual Solution Decisions back on The People and The Business. This is a continuous act of balancing back and forth between The People, The Business, and The Solution to achieve a Winning Solution after many Solution Iterations and interactions with stakeholders.

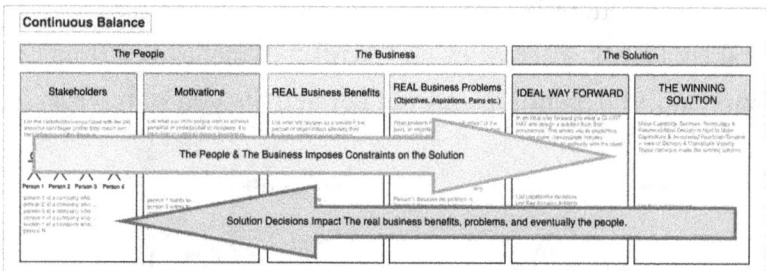

Diagram11 - www.SD2win.com/diagram11

How can you share and collaborate on this artifact within the team or all relevant internal stakeholders?

When the entire solution team is in one place, this is a great artifact to print on a wall at A1 size and use sticky notes to keep updating over the period of the deal.

In a real world context, teams are often distributed across different countries, especially for large solutions.

Following are some of the key aspects that would be required by a tool that hosts this artifact:

- The collaboration required for this artifact works best when it is **live** during calls or meetings with remote teams.
- It is important to have offline collaborations as well as often not every team member will be operating in the same time zone.
- A robust versioning to view changes over time when needed and the ability to roll back changes is necessary.
- Having the ability to collaborate from anywhere and any device is critical, as well.

Keeping all the above in mind, Google Docs is currently the best place to hold Artifact 0 as it meets all the requirements.

An alternative to Google Docs is Microsoft Word online. It offers similar versatility of collaboration but not of versioning.

I will keep on experimenting with what are the best tools for Artifact 0. You can follow this topic at <u>SD2win.com/Artifact0</u>.

This is the link for the artifact on Google Docs: <u>bit.ly/SSDFAR0</u> for your use.

Succinctly, Artifact 0 is extremely important in the context of large teams because you will have a shared view of the solution in one place - the same place where your sales team, your solution team, and your delivery and operation team go to view the current state of the solution. It is like the North Star of a solution; it guides all team members and helps them navigate the information they need for the solution. It also helps onboarding new solution team members in a fast and consistent manner around the solution.

Section 6: Limitless Possibilities

6.1 Clarity of a Decision-Driven System without the Rigidity That Stifles Innovation

Now you know about the Simple Solution Framework. Effectively, it is Solution Iterations and Interactions with Stakeholder. You exit a Solution Iteration at any point of time to get feedback and progress your Solution Design. The key measure for a successful Solution Iteration Exit is to maintain or increase your level of empathy and credibility with your customer or stakeholder. That will allow you to qualify better and amplify your credibility and influence to eventually maximize your chances to win.

You use Artifact 0 to record information resulting from every Solution Iteration or every interaction with a stakeholder. You also use Artifact 0 as a dashboard to access all Solution Artifacts. Artifact 0 will allow you to streamline internal communications and provide a shared end-to-end picture bringing all team members from sales to solution architecture to delivery and operations closer together. Artifact 0 brings non-customer facing team members as close to the customer as they can get. The use of Artifact 0 allows you to move fast with your team, which in turn will maximize your chances to win.

This framework gives a clear model toward Solution Design to Win that allows you to have a better conversation internally with your team and internal stakeholders. Further, the same model allows you to have better, more relevant conversations with your customers. This framework gives you the strategy and the tactics to connect with your client at a different level, to differentiate yourself from the pack, and to put forward a Winning Solution.

The power of this system is that it is Decision Driven and it does not stifle innovation by rigid steps to follow. Instead, it focuses on key activities to ensure everyone is working towards the same objective. That is what allows this system to deliver results.

The following three pictures summarize the framework.

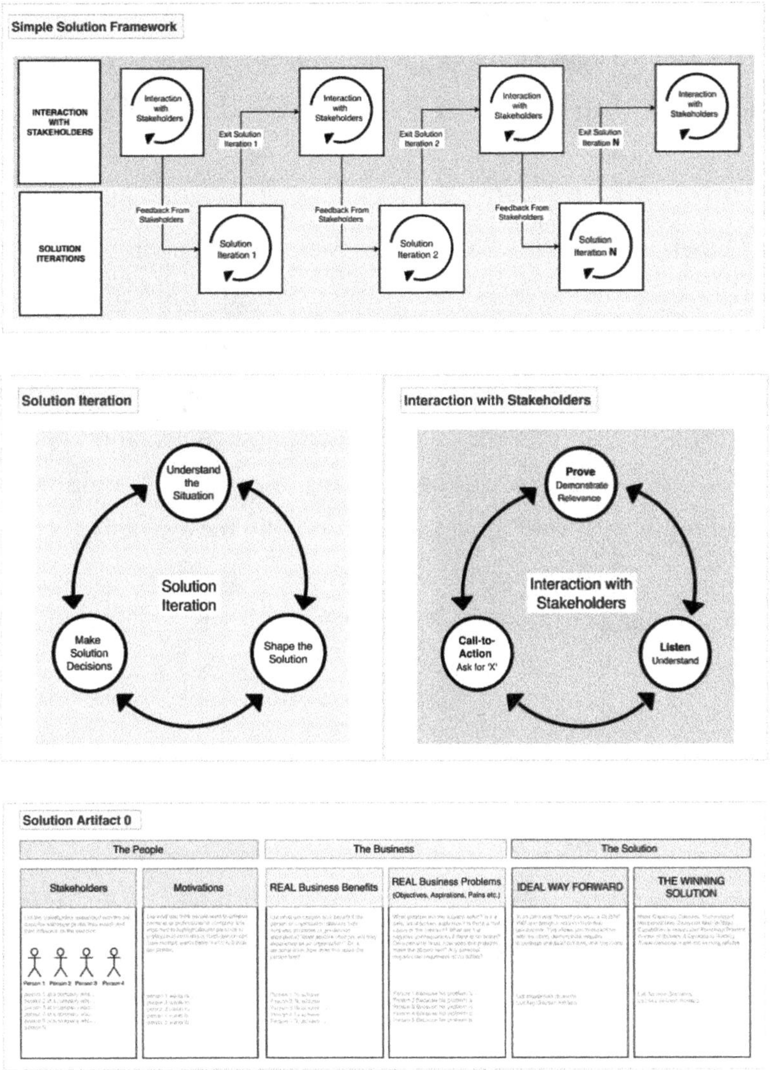

Diagram12 - www.SD2win.com/diagram12

The secret concepts described earlier in the book go hand-in-hand with the Simple Solution Framework. It has been clearly described when to use these concepts in the context of a solution design process.

Following the Simple Solution Framework gives you the method to focus on what is wildly important for yourself and the client without missing the big picture. This will minimize waste and free up some of your time to have more meaningful conversations with internal stakeholders, partners, and clients to ensure maximum alignment. This, in turn, will build your credibility with your customers so you will have an influencing authority when big decisions are about to happen. Eventually, the solutions you design will consistently win and help your customer win, building sustainable businesses.

One of the reasons why I wrote this book is because I felt strongly I could help others with this topic and share this knowledge I was lucky to accumulate because I worked around great people, mentors, colleagues, peers, and customers who allowed me to understand better what is really needed in the space of B2B Solution Design. This book was possible thanks to them and their experiences, and thanks to every person who helped me along the way.

With this book, I feel there is a continuous sharing of knowledge to help at least one more person gain a great insight, become better at what they do, or to inspire a whole department, organization or company to operate better at B2B Solution Design helping build sustainable businesses.

You picked up this book for a reason. Whatever your motivation is, learn something new, design Winning Solutions, get better at your job, minimize waste, maximize free time, and help build sustainable solutions and businesses making a lasting impression on the world. The key is to take action! The following section gives you a path of what to do next.

6.2 How to Get the Most out of this book

To get the most of out of this book, I recommend three things:

1. **Learn:** Read the book and understand the framework. Download and review the resources mentioned in the book to understand the framework better. Subscribe to get the latest articles, artifacts, and resources at SD2Win.com/NewArticles. Some of the articles will provide you with practical elements, examples, sample Solution Artifacts, how to stay organized to win, what tools to use for what, etc. Use them!
2. **Experiment:** Take your solution through the framework as you read this book. Use the resources and the artifacts in the book and the extended links.
3. **Pilot:** Get the Team involved, make The Simple Solution Framework system work for you and your environment!

Congratulations as you have just finished reading this book, which puts you in the top 20% of those who take action and follow through. Now it is time to keep momentum and decide today to win without losing, to design better solutions, to help build sustainable businesses, to minimize waste and maximize time for your work or your family.

Take Action! The door is open. The decision to enter is yours.

I am always happy to listen or support. For any queries or feedback or results of your pilot or experimentation with The Simple Solution Framework, you can email me at <u>Hassan@SD2Win.com</u> or add your feedback here: <u>SD2Win.com/Feedback</u>.

In closing, life is short, and you have shared some of your precious time with me by reading this book. Thank you.

I hope you have enjoyed reading this book!

Don't forget to check out the bonus material and resources associated with this book.

Bonus Material

I've compiled practical material I think you'll find as an incredibly useful addition to some of the key ideas discussed in this book.

Steer Away from Talking About the Solution:
SD2Win.com/ToolsToSteerAwayFromTalkingSolution - At this link, you can download and read practical conversation tools i.e. statements, sentences, questions and examples to help you steer away from talking about the solution and shift focus to the business.

Solution Artifacts
SD2Win.com/SolutionArtifacts - At this link, you can find and download a list of artifacts, sample or template artifacts as well as examples of Solution Artifacts you can re-use for designing your solution (The content will be available late in 2019. When you add your email, you will receive the article straight in your inbox once published.)

Solution Types
SD2Win.com/SolutionTypes - At this link, you can learn about Solution Types in more detail. Solution Types will help you make it simpler to communicate within the organization what solution type you are going for and to get a common under-

standing around what types of practical artifacts each solution type includes or excludes (The content will be available late in 2019. When you add your email, you will receive the article straight in your inbox once published.)

Organized To Win

SD2Win.com/OrganizedToWin - At this link, you can learn about all Solution Design tools - what tools to use when, why and how to use it in the context of Solution Design (The content will be available late in 2019. When you add your email, you will receive the article straight in your inbox once published.)

URGENT PLEA!

Finally, thank you for taking the time to read this book!

I really appreciate your feedback, and I love hearing what you have to say.

I need your input to make the next version of this book and my future books better.

Please leave me a helpful review on Amazon, letting me know what you thought of the book and how it helped you gain an insight, learn something new, get better at what you do or design winning solutions. I can't wait to connect with you.

Many thanks!

Hassan Nasser
Hassan@SD2Win.com

Resources - Solution Design to Win

Graphs, Diagrams, and Pictures

SD2Win.com/Diagrams - At this link, you can find graphs, diagrams, and pictures used in the book in high resolution to print them, share them and use them as you see fit.

Steer Away from Talking About the Solution

SD2Win.com/ItsNotAboutTheNail - At this link, you can find a cool video to conceptualize steering away from talking about the solution.

Simple Solution Framework - Artifact 0

SD2win.com/Artifact0 - At this link, you can find Artifact 0 for you to copy, print, share and use. Also, possible updates on tools to hold artifact 0 will be published here.

Solution Design to Win Articles

SD2Win.com/NewArticles - At this link, you can register to all new articles to be published in association with the practice of Solution Design to Win.

Stakeholders' Buying Personas

SD2Win.com/TypicalStakeholdersPersonas - At this link, you can find details about stakeholders personas typically involved in a B2B deal as well as their role in the buying cycle. You can reuse, update, and make your own.

Reading List

SD2Win.com/ReadingList - At this link, you can find the list of all book recommendations associated with this topic in one place. I will continuously update this list.

Key Terms and Concepts

SD2Win.com/KeyTermsConcepts - At this link, you can find the summary list of key terms and concepts discussed in this book with a small description and reference to where you can find them in the book.

Feedback

SD2Win.com/Feedback - At this link, you can give me any feedback.

SD2Win.com/4LevelProofSystem - At this link, you can give me feedback specific to the 4-Level Proof System.

Notes

Sales Ratios and Benchmarks
Here are some references for Sales Ratios and benchmarks I used.

https://www.propellercrm.com/blog/sales-benchmark-rates
https://www.hubspot.com/sales-close-rate
https://www.rainsalestraining.com/blog/average-sales-win-rates-how-do-you-compare
https://blog.hubspot.com/sales/new-sales-close-rate-industry-benchmarks-how-does-your-close-rate-compare

Emotional Buying Decisions
Following is a link associated with the topic of buying decisions you might find useful.

https://www.inc.com/logan-chierotti/harvard-professor-says-95-of-purchasing-decisions-are-subconscious.html

Active Listening
Following are some links associated with the topic of active listening you might find useful.

https://www.ted.com/talks/julian_treasure_5_ways_to_listen_better/transcript?referrer=playlist-great_ted_talks_for_language_practice&language=en#t-7643

https://www.the1thing.com/blog/the-one-thing/mastering-nonjudgmental-communication/

https://www.mindtools.com/CommSkll/ActiveListening.htm

https://study.com/academy/lesson/the-difference-between-reflective-active-listening.html

www.ingramcontent.com/pod-product-compliance
Lightning Source LLC
Chambersburg PA
CBHW071700200326
41519CB00012BA/2574